G000144587

It was

I was

In

Well, where would <u>you</u> go for your day trip?

So I woke up, bright-eyed and bushy-tailed, and announced to my wife of five days:

"Happy Christmas! We're going to Bethlehem!"

Bethlehem was only seven miles from our Jerusalem guesthouse. Lucy and I would get to stand there and imagine a pregnant woman and her husband arriving 2,000 years ago, right there in those streets, looking for somewhere to stay as the labour pains started.

We'd get to look at the fields and imagine the shepherds out there with their sheep, in those very fields.

It would be marvellous. What could go wrong?

Here's what went wrong.

I had forgotten that there was a wall in the way.

I hadn't really thought through the politics of the Middle East as I organised the trip or made our Christmas Day plans. With everything else that was going on with the wedding and honeymoon arrangements, I'd forgotten that there's a wall between Jerusalem and Bethlehem, between Israel and the West Bank. Built in 2003, it is in most places at least 8 metres high. It stretches for 485 miles. And it is a major obstacle if you are trying to get from Jerusalem to Bethlehem with your bride on Christmas Day.

We queued for hours. Guards with guns patrolled the lines. Happy Christmas!

I think you could say it sucked the romance out of the day a bit.

THIS IS WHY IT MATTERS

I don't know if you've ever spent Christmas in a strange place. That's certainly the weirdest location for Christmas morning I've ever ended up in—standing at the place that perhaps best sums up one of this world's most insurmountable divisions.

Right now, as you read this booklet, there's still a wall between Jerusalem and Bethlehem. And right now, there are walls between couples, between siblings, between parents and children—walls running through lounges as families gather (or don't gather) for Christmas. Maybe you're all too painfully aware of the relational wall separating members of your family. That's the reality. We cover it with tinsel, turkey and TV. But even at Christmas—sometimes, especially at Christmas—this is a world of walls.

Jesus—God's own Son—left heaven to come into this world.

He was born in an animal shelter in Bethlehem because a Roman emperor whose armies were occupying Israel decided to send everyone back to their home towns for a census.

His parents would have shared the road from Nazareth to Bethlehem with occupying soldiers.

He was born into a reality not so different from the reality of today's world.

So this booklet isn't going to tell the story of Christmas. Most of us have appeared in (and, if you're a parent, sat through) enough Nativity plays to know the outline of the story: Mary, Gabriel, pregnancy, Bethlehem, baby Jesus, manger, shepherds, angels, wise men, gold, frankincense and myrrh.

That's the story of Christmas—but I want to focus on the *significance* of Christmas—which, ironically, becomes easier and easier to miss the more and more familiar the story sounds to us.

And, standing there at that wall, I realised: This, *right here,* is why Christmas matters. At the first Christmas, Jesus was born to join us on this earth not because everything here is great and he wanted to join the party. No—he came because things are not as they should be in this world of walls.

THE REASON FOR THE WALLS

The first Christmas was an utterly supernatural event. It involved angels—who, by the way, are powerful spiritual beings who act as God's messengers, rather than small girls dressed in a white sheet with a tinsel-based headband. And when God sent an angel to

Mary's fiancé, Joseph, to tell him what was about to happen, the angel told him:

> *"[Mary] will give birth to a son, and you are to give him the name Jesus, because he will save his people from their sins." (The Gospel of Matthew, chapter 1, verse 21)*

That message diagnosed the reason for the walls in our world. The word "sins" sums up what's gone wrong. Sins are not just doing things that are a bit wrong, or even very wrong. Sins are the actions and attitudes that spring from a decision to reject the loving authority of the God who made all things. That's the sin that lies beneath all sins. It's the choice to live without a relationship with our Maker—to say to him, "This is my life, and I will live by my rules". Sin is taking all that God gives—life, breath, friendship, love, fun—and ignore, or abuse, the Giver.

It's the choice to live, as the Bible puts it, "alienated from God and … enemies in your mind" (Colossians 1 v 21). Though we don't tend to think of it this way, we choose conflict—war—with the God who made us and gives us everything we have.

Right now, there is a wall in each of our hearts. It's a wall we build to keep God out—to keep him off the throne of our lives, so that we can carry on saying, in effect, "My life, my rules".

And that's what builds all the other walls. The Bible says that, from the very first rejection of God back in the mists of human history, turning our backs on God means turning our backs on each other. John Stuart Mill, one of the fathers of modern liberalism and economic theory, was on to something when he wrote back in the nineteenth century:

"We are self-seeking individuals looking to maximise the optimum benefit for ourselves from every decision."

This is what we're like. Putting ourselves rather than God at the centre of our lives—looking to maximise the optimum benefit for ourselves—damages our relationships with humanity. Sin constructs a wall between ourselves and our God—and between ourselves and each other. It runs between peoples, along borders; and it runs between people, within workplaces and families and homes.

I didn't grow up in a Christian home, but as a teenager I realised that something was badly wrong, both with me and with the world. It actually came as quite a relief to discover what the problem was: the truth that I sin, because humanity sins.

And I remember being struck by this truth on honeymoon that Christmas Day as we waited at the wall.

I mentioned it to Lucy. It didn't improve the romantic atmosphere very much.

WAR IS OVER (EXCEPT IT ISN'T)

The wall in our own hearts explains why we can't tear down the walls in our own lives and throughout our world. It explains why we just don't seem able to stop the wars, end all poverty and guarantee justice.

Over 45 years ago, John Lennon wished us a "Happy Xmas" and promised us that "War Is Over (If You Want It)". Well, more than 45 Christmases have passed, and the wars have never stopped, however much we all want them to.

7

WHY?

When we reject relationship with God and reject the good, wise rule of God in our lives, it damages our relationships. You don't need me to tell you how that looks on a personal level—so many of us know the pain, the regret and the sadness all too well. And on a geopolitical level, it looks like walls between people—be it Hadrian's Wall, the Berlin Wall, or the one between Jerusalem and Bethlehem.

Truth is, it's no better in the world of religion, either. Maybe that's what puts you off church. There's a photograph that sums up the religious walls that our sin can build—a photo of two churches, in an English town, right next to each other. In the middle of the 1800s, there was such an angry falling out in the congregation of St Mary's in Stoke Newington that half of them went directly next door and built their own church. So there are these two churches, right next to one another, and they stand as a reminder of the way humanity is so very good at allowing division and causing conflict, and so very bad at ending disputes and finding peace.

Happy Christmas!

But keep reading—keep listening to the message of the angel. We've seen how he summed up the *problem* in one word—sins. He also described the *solution* in another single word…

SAVE

"He will save his people from their sins."

Christmas is not about us having a happy day while ignoring the problem; it is about God getting involved in human history to solve the problem. (And when you grasp that, Christmas Day becomes truly happy.)

At the first Christmas, God's Son became a man. Jesus lived a perfect life. Jesus never rejected his Father, our Creator. Yet at the other end of his earthly life from lying in the manger, Jesus died hanging on a cross. And he did that in order to experience the misery of complete separation from his Father that we have chosen by rejecting relationship with him. He died to bring us forgiveness so that we could enjoy coming into friendship with God—not just in this life, but for ever. Jesus came to save people from the consequences of their sin. He came to break down the walls we build between ourselves and our God. He came to announce that, in the most cosmic, most eternal, and most significant sense:

"War Is Over (If You Want It)."

Happy Christmas!

And once the wall between us and God is broken down by his forgiveness of us, and we're at peace with our Creator, we can start to break down the other walls with the same dynamite—the dynamite of forgiveness.

HOW TO ENJOY PEACE

There are two great things about being a pastor at Christmastime. The first is that you get lots of presents, including some hilarious ones. One year, someone gave me a bright pink jumper. Another, someone gave me a dog bowl. (I don't have a dog.)

The second is that you get to choose what you talk about at carol services and no one can stop you. So last year, I picked a Bible verse that sounds as if it has nothing to do with Christmas. I chose it because I think that in fact it has *everything* to do with Christmas. It's this:

> *"Bear with each other and forgive one another if any of*
> *you has a grievance against someone. Forgive as the Lord*
> *forgave you." (Colossians 3 v 13)*

If you want to experience peace this Christmas… if there's a wall between you and someone else and you would love it to come down… you need to grasp this verse.

Christmas is a time of great joy and also of great reflection. It's a time when the good things in life are seen clearest, but also when the walls and the regrets and the mistakes and unful-filled hopes loom largest. So many of us can't wait for Christmas, but others of us can't wait to get through it. Most of us enjoy it and yet, at the same time, we have a tinge of sadness about some element of it—and often that sadness is caused by the knowledge that, to some extent and in one way or another, we've put up walls.

Maybe it's a wall between a married couple who've stopped really talking to one another or listening to one another. Each is waiting for the other partner to change—then they'll dismantle the wall (maybe).

Maybe it's a wall between a parent and a child, where both feel let down or not listened to or unappreciated or unloved by the other.

Maybe it's a wall between two old friends, where a forgotten birthday or a lack of phone calls or a shortage of sympathy at some point has seen everything go cold.

How can we change? How can this Christmas really be one of peace and love and joy?

Only if it's a Christmas of forgiveness. And you get the power to forgive, and to ask others to forgive you, by seeing what God was doing the first Christmas, in the coming of Jesus.

"Forgive as the Lord forgave you."

So here are the three steps to taking down the walls.

1. You realise that actually Jesus really was born in Bethlehem. Christianity has historical clothes. It's not based on a philosophy or a mantra or a feeling. It's based on historical events. It happened in Bethlehem, in the town I finally stood in, after the hours of queueing at the wall that Christmas Day. It happened, as the carol puts it, "once in royal David's city". Jesus really walked the roads of Israel, just as I did on honeymoon. He really did die on a cross—and, yes, he really did rise again from death.

   And of course, this may be more than you're willing to accept right now, because as you think about it you find it very hard to believe. Well, that's good—what matters is to think about it, and to look into the evidence for these events. Please do! It may be stronger than you've been thinking. But for the moment, please read on—because seeing what effect it would have if this were all true will motivate you to find out if it really is true.

2. You realise the meaning of what happened in history—that Jesus came to help you, to save you and to change you. You understand that he was born because he loves you and that he died because he wants to forgive you.

3. You accept what you are being offered—forgiveness from God and friendship with God. You say,

> *"Yes, God, this is for me. This is what Christmas, and life, is going to be all about. I want to say to you, 'My life, your rules'. I want to admit my sin, and to accept and enjoy your forgiveness. I want to be at peace with you, rather than at war with you."*

And so you walk through life knowing that the most important wall has come down; and that the most important Person in the universe loves you. You're forgiven by the Lord, and now you're in a position to begin to "forgive as the Lord forgave you". C.S. Lewis, who became a Christian in his thirties and went on to write the Narnia books, put it like this:

> *"To be Christian means to forgive the indefensible in other people because God has forgiven the indefensible in you."*

In many ways, true Christianity looks like forgiveness.

STILL WITH US

Jesus doesn't only call us to forgive, or even merely show us how to forgive—he empowers his friends to forgive.

At the first Christmas, Jesus was given a nickname:

> *"'The virgin will conceive and give birth to a son, and they will call him Immanuel' (which means 'God with us')." (Matthew 1 v 23)*

"God with us"—that's the nickname. As we look in that manger in history, we can say, *There was God— Immanuel—come to be with people.* But it's even better than that, because Jesus can be with us today. At the other end of his time on earth, after he'd risen and before he returned to rule in heaven, Jesus promised his friends:

> *"Surely I am with you always, to the very end of the age."*
> *(Matthew 28 v 20)*

The God who lived on earth 2,000 years ago now lives with his people through his Spirit. C.S. Lewis did not forgive others through his own efforts. He forgave because he had God with him: the Spirit changing him. If you know you need to forgive, or ask for forgiveness… if you know you need to give up that anger, stop replaying that wrong, cease plotting your revenge… if you know a wall needs taking down… you need to look *back* at God's Son, and see that he came to be with you and forgive you. You need to accept his offer of friendship. And then you need to look *in* at God's Spirit coming to be with you and empower you.

The Bible makes clear that the Christian faith is not just about believing in a Creator God who is way up there. It's not just about looking back to the figure of Jesus, who lived centuries ago, way back then. The essence of life as a Christian is not God's distance from us, but God's presence with us, by his Spirit, so we can enjoy his forgiveness and reach out to others in forgiveness.

The 18th-century English poet Alexander Pope wrote, "To err is human; to forgive, divine". God knows that, and so he sends his Spirit to strengthen us, to melt our hearts, and to enable us to say two phrases that will be at the heart of any truly peace-filled Christmas. Here they are:

"I'm sorry, I was wrong—please forgive me."

"That's OK. I forgive you."

It may take time. It may take patience. It may even be that the door keeps being slammed in your face despite your request for or offer of forgiveness. (And if that happens, then at least you'll be able to appreciate a little more how God's Son, having come at the first Christmas, felt to be greeted, in large part, by indifference and opposition.) But these are the first steps. These are the basis of a truly peace-filled Christmas. And you'll only find the motivation to forgive others, and to ask for forgiveness from others, as you ask for and find forgiveness from God—in other words, you will "forgive" as you appreciate how "the Lord forgave you."

PEACE ON EARTH

The angels were busy at the first Christmas. After Jesus had been born, a whole choir's-worth of angels appeared in those fields outside Bethlehem. And here's what they said:

"Glory to God in the highest heaven, and on earth peace to those on whom his favour rests." (Luke 2 v 14)

"On earth peace." This is Christmas—the message of the first Christmas and the reason for the first Christmas. War is over,

whatever you've done, if you want it to be. The wall between you and God will be torn down by his forgiveness if you ask for it. And that's what will enable you to start to dismantle the other walls in life, helped by God's Spirit working in you, as you say:

"I'm sorry, I was wrong—please forgive me."

"That's OK. I forgive you."

This Christmas, will you ask God to take down the wall in your heart, so that you can take down the walls in your life?

WHAT NEXT?

Thanks for reading! It's worth asking yourself: What will I do next?

To keep considering Christianity's message, the best things to do are:

1. *Read a Gospel*—a historical account of the life of Jesus, found in the Bible. There are four: Matthew, Mark, Luke and John.

2. *Pray.* Speak to God (even if you're not sure he's there) and ask him to help you see the reality of who he is and who you are.

You may also like to go to christianityexplored.org to find answers to questions, and hear from people who've become Christians.

Perhaps, though, you're reading this having just asked God to take down the wall in your heart—you've prayed something like the prayer on page 12. That's great! I'd encourage you to find a church that bases all it says and does on the Bible… to start praying… and to start listening to God in the Bible. If you'd like help with any of that, I'd love to hear from you—just email info@thegoodbook.co.uk. Thanks again for reading.

It was Christmas Day.
I was on honeymoon.
In Jerusalem.
Well, where would <u>you</u> go
for your day trip?

thegoodbook
COMPANY

thegoodbook.com | .co.uk

ISBN 978-1-78498-349-9

9 781784 983499

Holidays / Christmas & Advent

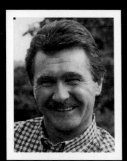

KEVIN WOODFORD'S
60 Best Recipes

I would like to express my thanks to the
following people who have made the
publication of this book possible.
To Barbara Dixon and Polly Powell of
HarperCollins for their foresight and
encouragement; to Jane Lush, Editor, BBC
Holiday Programme, for giving me the best
job on TV; to Bill Dale of Brookvale
Publications for being able to read my
writing; to Jane Middleton, my editor, for
such attention to detail and great patience; to
Michelle Garrett and Jacqueline Clark for the
evocative photographs, and to my family –
Steven, Janine and my wife Jean for being
there once again.

First published in 1997 by
HarperCollins*Publishers*, London

10 9 8 7 6 5 4 3 2 1

Editor: *Jane Middleton*
Food photographer: *Michelle Garrett*
Home economist: *Jacqueline Clark*

For HarperCollins*Publishers*
Commissioning Editor: *Barbara Dixon*
Designer and Illustrator: *Clare Baggaley*

A catalogue record for this book is available
from the British Library

ISBN 0 00 414013 3

Printed and bound in Great Britain

After gaining a B.A. from Hull
University, Kevin Woodford began
his working life as Head of
Department in a College of Further
Education. He then embarked on a
career as a chef, which took him to
many of Europe's top restaurants,
and he has also undertaken food
consultancy roles in the USA and
for the Bulgarian Government.

Kevin's communication skills led
him to a five-year contract with

Kevin Woodford

BBC Radio Sheffield, where he co-hosted a weekly live spot. Offers to work in television followed – as presenter of 'The Reluctant Cook' for the BBC; 'Microwave Maestro' and 'The Flying Cook' for Granada's 'This Morning' show; and guest appearances on many other television shows.

More recently, Kevin has proved to be a huge success on the BBC's 'Ready Steady Cook' and 'Can't Cook, Won't Cook', and as a presenter on the 'Holiday' programmes on BBC1.

His previous books include *The Reluctant Cook*, *Microwave Maestro*, *The Flying Cook* and *Surprise Chefs*. He is also a regular columnist for *Airlines of Britain* magazine. When Kevin is not travelling the world as a TV presenter, he lives with his family on the Isle of Man.

Contents

𝒮pain

𝒢reece

France

Italy

Portugal

Introduction

Gone are the days when the Mediterranean was a far-off land, full of alien inhabitants and even more alien food. Nowadays it's not unusual for a British pantry to be stocked with extra virgin olive oil, oak-aged balsamic vinegar and sun-dried tomato paste. We have all grown up and our palates have acquired a certain sophistication. Thanks to a surge in package tourism and the sudden growth of the restaurant culture, our eyes and appetites have widened to the sights, smells and tastes of Europe.

So, now we know our feta from our fusilli, the next stage is to appreciate the full range of cooking styles and the ease with which they can be recreated at home. Once you've tried a few of the recipes in this book, you'll discover that good food is not as hard to prepare as it looks. In no time your friends will be congratulating you on the tremendous efforts you've clearly made at a dinner party. You'll thank them, saying it

was nothing, and only you'll know what was involved.

In this book I have put together a few of my favourite dishes from Greece, Spain, Italy, France and Portugal. Some will seem familiar, others less so, but all will surprise you in some small way. The biggest shock of all will be how simple it is to achieve excellence. So loosen your belt, broaden your mind and tuck in!

Greece

Greek islands have long served as magnets for summer funseekers in pursuit of glorious sunshine, crumbling old columns and ancient Greek tragedies – and I don't mean the food. The damage done to Greece's culinary reputation by the greasy kebabs sold from vans and takeaways across Britain almost exceeds the bloodshed at the fall of Troy. Greek food, in truth, is excellent – loads of fresh fruit and vegetables, a fantastic variety of fish and shellfish, lamb, pork, goat and chicken. The horror

stories of overcooked Greek food, left to go cold and swimming in oil, are simply unfair. One belief that we do have to suspend, however, is that good food should be piping hot. Greek cooks choose to serve dishes tepid, firmly believing that hot food is bad for the soul – or at least the digestion. And there is no doubt that flavours are indistinguishable at a searing 30°C. If you want to savour aubergines, lamb and cheese cooked in the traditional manner, then lukewarm moussaka – trust me – is a must.

The thing I love about Greek tavernas is their eagerness to welcome anyone into the kitchen to have a look at what's going on. I always have a good old nose around the pots to see what's cooking before deciding what to eat. This is definitely the best way of acquainting yourself with local dishes. The menu in most tavernas bears absolutely no relation to the dishes they cook. This is because they collect standard menu cards palmed off on them by big wine merchants who have something to promote. If you really want to taste the speciality of the house, toss the menu away and ask the proprietor, 'What's good today?' I don't know about you but I'm the first to hit the phrasebook, and I've learned this line off by heart.

Spain

Food is approached with much gusto in Spain. Meals tend to be family affairs, big shared production numbers, prepared lovingly and enjoyed slowly. Cooks go for freshness rather than complexity, and stick to local ingredients, which is why regional cooking still thrives. From the deserted uplands of Almería to the leafy Asturias, the country spans such a huge variety of landscapes that it's no wonder the cuisine is so wide-ranging. Anyone who thinks Spain stops at the suntraps of the costas should try a wet weekend in Galicia, where they would find themselves swapping chilled gazpacho and olive oil for warming wild boar and pork fat.

To taste Spain's unique combination of wholesome rusticity and Old World exotica, your best bet would be to gatecrash a family paella. Originally a peasant dish, paella, named after the wide shallow vessel in which it is cooked, has remained a favourite for centuries. Ingredients are all there on the doorstep – fresh fish and seafood, chicken, succulent peppers, saffron and, of course, rice. Rice is the most widely planted cereal in the world but it is not exactly native to Spain. It first turned up in the Iberian Peninsula courtesy of the Moors in the 8th century and has been growing prolifically in the provinces of Valencia and Andalucía ever since. Valencian mothers first cooked paella for their families on Sundays and since then it has elbowed its way into the repertoires of professional chefs nationwide. It's still a dish to be shared and is sure to create a relaxed atmosphere at even the most formal dinner party.

Italy

Italians love food. It's a profound devotion that has been nurtured through the centuries to become an all-consuming passion. Their predecessors, the ancient Romans, were traditionally given to excesses of gluttony at their orgiastic feasts. Their modern counterparts haven't inherited the taste for fried dormice, swan's intestines or pickled pheasant brains. In fact, modern Italian food, once considered stodgy and high in cholesterol, is now generally thought to be the healthiest diet in Europe. Plenty of pulses, fresh ingredients, and olive oil rather than butter does Italians the world of good. In the South they keep especially trim, with lots of scrumptious fruit and vegetables and loads of fresh fish. Often, three generations of one family live together in one house, and recipes are handed down in every household – usually from mamma. It's a bit of a cliché but any Italian is sure to tell you that their country's cooking is the best in the world and – without pausing for breath – that their mother's is the finest example of all.

France

When one thinks of France, one thinks of designer clothes, designer homes and – let's face it – they're to blame for designer food. France is Europe's culinary catwalk, and is notoriously smug about its cuisine.

However, in the fashion-conscious Seventies, disaster struck. France did itself a bit of a disservice when it created *nouvelle cuisine*. The trend, which was widely misinterpreted, appeared to call for minuscule portions in bizarre combinations arranged artistically on a plate – a slither of steak with half a strawberry was considered the business, but it left everyone half-famished. Now we've survived the famine, *nouvelle cuisine* is out and hearty country cooking back in.

If France has a problem it is that its culinary reputation is hard to live up to. Foodies flock to Provence in search of the famed *bouillabaisse,* to Burgundy to hunt down the authentic *coq au vin*, and to the Languedoc to sample the celebrated *cassoulet*. Clutching on to romanticized notions of French fare, visitors to the country can be disappointed when they find that the cookbook clichés aren't immediately forthcoming. But let yourself be inspired by a few good ideas – from a cookbook not unlike this one, perhaps – and you may never feel let down again.

Portugal

For summer tourists, Portugal is a mecca of golden beaches, whitewashed villas, manicured golf courses and, everywhere you look, those ornately decorated tiles. Stuck out on the far side of Europe, this long slender country, stretching 580 km (360 miles) from north to south and hugging the western edge of Spain, is home to 10 million, and is one of the smallest countries in Europe. Skinny and small though it may be, the land is mountainous and spans enough latitude to produce differences in climate, and hence a variety of foods. But it's not the lie of the land that is solely responsible for the food. Throughout its history of foreign invasions, Portugal has adopted cultural influences from all over the world. Invaded by the Phoenicians (who brought saffron and planted vines), the Greeks, Visigoths and Romans (who are to thank for their forests of olive trees and wonderfully fruity olive oils), the Portuguese have nonetheless kept a firm grip on their own culture, and have survived the recent tourist invasion with remarkable calm.

The coastal region of Portugal was dominated by the Moors for over 500 years and it shows. Garlands of bougainvillaea adorn whole villages of typical Moorish domed buildings, with their whitewashed arches and traditional latticed chimneys. Portuguese desserts are also undeniably Moorish. *Pastelerias* are everywhere to entice you with delicious sweets based on egg yolks, sugar and almonds. Convent nuns first created them and their bizarre names have stuck – such as the almond cake 'heavenly bacon', or the 'nun's belly' and 'angel's breast' marzipan sweets.

There's a quaint fable surrounding the almond trees that blanket southern Portugal with their stunning pinky-white blossom every winter. Legend tells of an ancient Moorish king who planted the vast expanses of almond forests as a substitute for snow. His Scandinavian bride longed so desperately for a glimpse of snow that he wanted to prevent her dying of a broken heart. A beautiful sentiment, a beautiful sight, but my guess is that she just liked to nibble on nuts!

Greece

In culinary terms, the Greek god is lamb. It's served minced, minted, off the bone, on the bone, steaked, spit-roasted, chopped and totally kebab-ed – but almost always cooked to perfection. As in most Mediterranean countries, vegetables tend to be treated like fruit and are usually served raw. Good chips, though. When you do chance upon a cooked vegetable it will be thoroughly drenched in calorific, albeit delicious, olive oil and fried to a crisp.

Fish, though adored and revered, is becoming so expensive that it now plays second fiddle to meat. For a land full of fishermen it is a tragedy that they've overfished their Aegean to the extent that it has become something of an Achilles heel. Who said there are plenty more fish in the sea? Yet fantastic fish dishes, simply baked, sautéed or grilled, can still be had – at a price. If you've ever been to the Dodecanese islands you may have been lucky enough to taste the coveted and glorious sea urchin roe. The reddish urchins are split and emptied and their roe, which reputedly has aphrodisiac qualities, is eaten raw. Squid and octopus are still in plentiful supply and, fresh from the sea, make a wonderful meal.

If you're a grazer or a nibbler, then the Greeks have got you sussed. Try the very Turkish-tasting *meze*. A protracted meal is made up of a selection of small starters, from humous and taramosalata to vine leaves, meatballs, squid, octopus and peppers, many of which are stuffed – which is exactly what you will be, long before the main course appears. But what a way to go. Vegetarians be warned – only the most tourist-conscious resorts will cater for you. There are some delicious standbys available everywhere, though – aubergine bakes, tzatziki, feta cheese salad, and that old faithful yoghurt and honey.

A holiday in the Greek islands should always include a plate of huge, sundrenched tomatoes stuffed to overflowing with lots of Mediterranean goodies, and this recipe has it all. The combination of mint and dill will immediately evoke memories of a past visit to Greece.

Domátes Yemistes

Stuffed Tomatoes

preparation time

15

minutes

cooking time

40 to *45*

minutes

serves *4*

8 as a starter,

as an accompaniment

Ingredients

8 large tomatoes

5 tablespoons virgin olive oil, plus extra for brushing

175 g (6 oz) shallots, finely diced

2 garlic cloves, crushed

1 tablespoon chopped fresh coriander

1 tablespoon chopped fresh mint

1 tablespoon chopped fresh dill

2 tablespoons pine nuts

125 g (4 oz) long grain rice, cooked

50 g (2 oz) mushrooms, finely diced

2 tablespoons tomato purée

1 glass of dry white wine

salt and freshly ground black pepper

1 Preheat the oven to 190°C, 375°F, gas mark 5.

2 Slice the tops off the tomatoes, carefully scoop out the flesh and set it aside for the stuffing.

3 Heat the oil in a frying pan, add the shallots and garlic and cook gently for 5 minutes, until softened.

4 Add the tomato flesh, herbs, pine nuts and salt and pepper, then cook gently for 6–8 minutes.

5 Stir the cooked rice, mushrooms, tomato purée and wine into the mixture. Check the seasoning and add more salt and pepper if necessary, then remove from the heat.

6 Fill the tomatoes with the mixture, brush them with a little olive oil and bake for 30 minutes. Serve straight away.

Kevin's Tip

The tomatoes used to make this in Greece tend to be large, distorted in shape, with uneven colouring and lots of ugly blemishes. But what wonderful flavours they have! In England I look for organically grown tomatoes. If they aren't in season, try the large beef tomatoes and concentrate even harder on developing the flavours of the filling.

Some fresh, crusty bread, a large glass of ouzo and a bowl of freshly made taramosalata. Utopia!

Taramosalata

Fish Roe Salad

preparation time

10

minutes

serves

4

1 Soak the bread in a little cold water, then squeeze it dry. Remove the skin from the fish roe.

2 Using a fork, mix the fish roe, onion and bread together until they become smooth and well blended (you could do this in a food processor or liquidizer for a smoother texture).

3 Gradually beat in the oil, followed by the lemon juice, and then season with salt and pepper. Chill until required.

Ingredients

4 slices of white bread, crusts removed

125 g (4 oz) smoked fish roe

50 g (2 oz) onion, finely diced

125 ml (4 fl oz) extra virgin olive oil

juice of 2 lemons

salt and freshly ground black pepper

Kevin's Tip

The great thing about making your own taramosalata is that you can adjust the proportions of the ingredients to suit your personal taste, especially the amount of oil.

On offer in every taverna, this salad varies greatly but feta, tomatoes, olives and lettuce are common denominators.

Horiátiki

Greek Salad

Ingredients

1 iceberg lettuce

6 shallots, finely diced

1 green pepper, halved, deseeded and diced

1 tablespoon chopped fresh coriander

1 tablespoon chopped fresh dill

500 g (1 lb) tomatoes, diced

½ cucumber, diced

12 green olives

250 g (8 oz) feta cheese, cut into cubes

6 anchovy fillets

4 tablespoons white wine vinegar

150 ml (5 fl oz) virgin olive oil

12 capers, rinsed

salt and freshly ground black pepper

preparation time 15 minutes

serves 6

1 Remove the outer leaves of the lettuce and discard. Shred the lettuce as finely as possible, then wash and pat dry. Place in a large bowl.

2 Add the shallots, green pepper, herbs, tomatoes, cucumber, olives, feta cheese and anchovy fillets. Gently mix together.

3 Whisk the vinegar into the oil and season with salt and pepper. Pour this dressing over the salad ingredients, add the capers and toss lightly until all the ingredients are coated with the dressing. Serve immediately.

I found this dish on one of Greece's liveliest islands. The town of Karthamena, 20 km (12 miles) from Kos, is popular with young Brits whose idea of a good holiday is to dance all night and sleep all day. The mussels are fried in a light, herby batter and make a delicious starter.

Míthia Tiganitá

Fried Mussels

preparation time
40
minutes

cooking time about
15
minutes

serves
4 to *6*

Ingredients

1 kg (2 lb) mussels

150 ml (5 fl oz) dry white wine

juice of 1 lemon

75 g (3 oz) plain flour

vegetable oil for deep-frying

salt and freshly ground black pepper

For the batter

2 eggs

75 g (3 oz) self-raising flour

½ teaspoon baking powder

a pinch of cayenne pepper

2 tablespoons chopped fresh dill

3 garlic cloves, crushed

Kevin's Tip

This dish is also lovely as a snack, served with a large bowl of garlic mayonnaise and plenty of fresh crusty bread.

1 Scrub the mussels under cold running water. Pull off the beards and scrape off any barnacles with a small sharp knife. Discard any open mussels that do not close when tapped lightly on a work surface.

2 Heat the wine in a large pan, add the mussels and cover with a tight-fitting lid. Cook over a medium-high heat for 3–5 minutes, until the mussels have opened.

3 Drain the mussels in a colander set over a medium saucepan to catch the cooking liquid. Discard any mussels that have remained closed. Remove the opened mussels from their shells and set aside to cool.

4 Add the lemon juice to the mussel cooking liquid and then boil it until it is reduced to half its volume. Check the seasoning and adjust if necessary.

5 To make the batter, lightly beat the eggs together. Sift the self-raising flour, baking powder and cayenne and whisk into the eggs until smooth. Add the dill and garlic and season with salt and pepper. Stir in 3–4 tablespoons of cold water to give a batter the consistency of single cream; beat until smooth.

6 Spread the plain flour over a plate and lightly coat the mussels in it, shaking off any surplus flour.

7 Heat some vegetable oil in a deep pan. Put the mussels in the batter a few at a time and then carefully place them in the hot oil. Fry for 2–3 minutes, until golden brown.

8 Drain the mussels on kitchen paper and keep warm while you cook the rest. Serve immediately, with a little of the reduced cooking liquid.

This simple recipe relies on the freshest possible ingredients, particularly the sardines, so that a perfect marriage of flavours can take place. Be sure to buy sardines that have not been previously frozen. Serve as a starter or a light meal.

Sarthelles sto Foúrno

Baked Sardines

preparation time

15

minutes

cooking time

30

minutes

serves

6

Ingredients

1 kg (2 lb) fresh sardines, cleaned and gutted

finely grated zest and juice of 1 lemon

6 garlic cloves, crushed

1 tablespoon chopped fresh dill

1 tablespoon chopped fresh parsley

125 ml (4 fl oz) dry white wine

salt and freshly ground black pepper

1 Preheat the oven to 180°C, 350°F, gas mark 4.

2 Rinse the sardines thoroughly and then pat them dry on kitchen paper. Place them in a lightly greased shallow baking dish large enough to hold them in a single layer.

3 Sprinkle the grated lemon zest, garlic, dill and parsley over the sardines, then season generously with salt and pepper.

4 Pour on the lemon juice and white wine, then cover the dish with a tight-fitting lid. Bake for 30 minutes or until the sardines are cooked through. Serve hot or warm.

Kevin's Tip

If, like me, you are conditioned to think that sardines should be cooked al fresco *on the barbecue, and this recipe appeals to you, then simply omit the white wine and follow your heart! Be sure to serve it with plenty of crusty white bread. This is a great help if you get those annoying little bones lodged in your mouth.*

I like to make this dish the day before serving to allow the flavours to infuse and then reheat it. It's substantial enough to serve as a vegetarian main course with crusty bread and a green salad, and also makes a good accompaniment to plain grilled meat or fish.

18

Melitzánes sto Foúrno

Baked Aubergines

preparation time

30

minutes, plus 30 minutes' salting the aubergines

cooking time

50

minutes

serves

6

Ingredients

1 kg (2 lb) large aubergines, thinly sliced

vegetable oil for shallow-frying

4 tablespoons extra virgin olive oil

175 g (6 oz) onions, thinly sliced

4 garlic cloves, crushed

1 tablespoon chopped fresh fennel herb

2 tablespoons chopped fresh basil

1 tablespoon chopped fresh oregano

750 g (1½ lb) tomatoes, skinned, deseeded and chopped (or use a 400 g/14 oz can of chopped tomatoes)

1 tablespoon tomato purée

1 glass of dry white wine

2 drops of Tabasco sauce

½ teaspoon Worcestershire sauce

a pinch of caster sugar

125 g (4 oz) fresh Parmesan cheese, grated

1 tablespoon chopped fresh parsley

salt and freshly ground black pepper

1 Put the aubergine slices on kitchen paper, sprinkle with salt and leave for 30 minutes.

2 Preheat the oven to 180°C, 350°F, gas mark 4. Rinse off the salt from the aubergines under cold running water, allowing the discoloured water to drain away. Gently pat the aubergines dry.

3 Heat a thin layer of vegetable oil in a large frying pan until very hot and add the aubergines (don't overcrowd the pan; cook them in batches if necessary). Season with salt and pepper and fry until golden on both sides. Transfer to a shallow ovenproof dish.

4 Heat the olive oil in a saucepan, add the onions and garlic and cook gently for 5 minutes, until softened. Stir in the herbs, tomatoes and tomato purée. Pour in the white wine and season with the Tabasco, Worcestershire sauce, sugar and some salt and pepper. Mix together well and simmer gently for 10 minutes.

5 Pour the sauce over the aubergines and sprinkle with the Parmesan cheese and parsley. Bake for 30–40 minutes, until golden brown on top, then serve immediately.

Kevin's Tip

Greek cheeses are readily available these days but I actually prefer the flavour of fresh Parmesan in this dish. It's well worth stealing an ingredient from another country in order to get a superb finish.

Pies of all sorts are an important element in the gastronomic history of Greece. For me, this spinach and feta pie brings back wonderful memories of a three-hour lunch in a quaint, whitewashed taverna, while sheltering from fierce midday sun on the unspoilt island of Lipsoi.

Spanakotyropitta

Spinach and Cheese Pie

preparation time
45
minutes

cooking time
40 to *50*
minutes

serves
4 to *6*

Ingredients

4 tablespoons olive oil

1 large onion, thinly sliced

75 g (3 oz) spring onions, finely diced

1 kg (2 lb) fresh spinach, washed

2 tablespoons chopped fresh dill

2 tablespoons chopped fresh parsley

4 eggs, beaten

250 g (8 oz) feta cheese, crumbled into small pieces

175 g (6 oz) butter, melted

500 g (1 lb) filo pastry

salt and freshly ground black pepper

Kevin's Tip

For an even more adventurous finish, try using more than one type of cheese but to the same quantity as in the recipe. Select cheeses with different tastes and textures.

1 Preheat the oven to 190°C, 375°F, gas mark 5.

2 Heat the oil in a deep pan, add the onion, spring onions and spinach and season with salt and pepper. Cook for 2 minutes.

3 Add the dill and parsley and cook, stirring constantly, for 2 minutes. Remove from the heat and leave to cool.

4 Mix together the eggs and feta. Using a slotted spoon, remove the spinach and onion mixture from the pan, leaving any liquid behind, and add to the eggs and cheese.

5 Use a little of the melted butter to grease a 25 cm (10 inch) flan tin with a removable base.

6 Lay a sheet of filo pastry out on a work surface and brush with melted butter, then put it over the base of the tin. Repeat with half the filo sheets, layering them over the base and sides of the tin and allowing them to overlap the sides. Keep the rest of the filo covered with cling film or a damp tea towel so it does not dry out.

7 Spread the filling evenly over the pastry and fold over the overlapping sheets of filo.

8 Brush the remaining sheets of filo with butter and arrange them on top of the filling, then pour over any remaining butter.

9 Bake the pie for 35–45 minutes, until well browned. Remove from the oven and leave to rest for 10 minutes, then cut into slices and serve.

This vegetarian version of one of the best-known Greek recipes is quite delightful. Feel free to vary the quantity of herbs to suit your taste. The stuffed vine leaves are further enhanced if you serve them with a simple sauce of Greek yoghurt with snipped chives and lemon juice stirred in.

Dolmathákia Latherá

tuffed Vine Leaves

preparation time
30
minutes, plus 30 minutes' soaking

cooking time
1
hour

serves
6

Ingredients

150 g (5 oz) long grain rice

250 g (8 oz) pack of preserved vine leaves

300 g (10 oz) onions, finely diced

3 tablespoons chopped fresh dill

3 tablespoons chopped fresh mint

2 tablespoons chopped fresh fennel herb

2 tablespoons chopped fresh parsley

juice of 1 lemon

150 ml (5 fl oz) extra virgin olive oil

300 ml (10 fl oz) boiling water

salt and freshly ground black pepper

1 Soak the rice in cold water to cover for 30 minutes.

2 Preheat the oven to 190°C, 375°F, gas mark 5.

3 Rinse the vine leaves in cold water and then place them in a bowl of hot water for 5 minutes. Carefully strain off the water, rinse the leaves with cold water again and then spread them over a large plate.

4 Drain the rice and mix it with the onions, herbs, half the lemon juice and half the olive oil. Season with salt and pepper.

5 Select any torn vine leaves and spread them over the base of a shallow ovenproof dish.

6 Put about a tablespoon of the filling on each remaining vine leaf, fold the bottom of the leaf over the filling, then fold in the sides and roll up to form a tight cylinder. Put them in the dish, making sure that they are packed tightly together.

7 Mix together the remaining oil and lemon juice, season with salt and pepper and pour on top of the stuffed vine leaves. Pour over the boiling water and cover with a lid.

8 Bake for 1 hour and then serve either hot or cold.

Kevin's Tip

If you decide to serve this dish cold, then be sure to use a good-quality olive oil. If you are using canned or bottled vine leaves, allow for a 350 g (12 oz) jar to yield about 50 leaves and do remember to allow for a little wastage due to torn leaves.

Surely this dish symbolizes Greece more than any other. If you choose to serve it for a dinner party it has the distinct advantage that it can be prepared in advance and then reheated when required. A good fishmonger will be more than happy to clean the squid for you.

Kalamárakia Yemistá

Stuffed Squid

preparation time
40
minutes

cooking time
1¼
hours

serves
6

Ingredients

6 small squid

75 ml (3 fl oz) olive oil

175 g (6 oz) onions, finely diced

2 garlic cloves, crushed

150 ml (5 fl oz) hot water

juice of 1 lemon

750 g (1½ lb) fresh spinach, washed and shredded

75 g (3 oz) long grain rice

2 tablespoons chopped fresh basil

1 tablespoon chopped fresh dill

salt and freshly ground black pepper

For the sauce

75 ml (3 fl oz) olive oil

300 g (10 oz) tomatoes, skinned, deseeded and chopped

1 tablespoon tomato purée

1 small glass of red wine

150 ml (5 fl oz) water

1. To prepare the squid, pull the head away from the body and discard the innards that come out with it, including the ink sac if there is one. Pull out the rest of the insides from the body – the translucent, plastic-like bone and, probably, some roe. Peel off the outer blue membrane from the body of the squid, then cut off and discard the fins. Wash the body thoroughly and pat dry.

2. Slice the tentacles from the head and discard the head. Wash the tentacles well and pat dry, then slice them finely.

3. To make the stuffing, heat the oil in a saucepan, then add the sliced tentacles and season with salt and pepper. Stir in the onions and garlic and cook for 5 minutes, until they have softened. Pour in the hot water and lemon juice, cover and cook gently for about 15–20 minutes.

4. Add the spinach, mix through and simmer for 5 minutes. Stir in the rice and cook for 5 minutes, then stir in the chopped herbs and season to taste with salt and pepper.

5. Pack the stuffing loosely into the body of the squid, leaving room for the rice to expand while cooking.

6. For the sauce, heat the oil in a wide saucepan, add the chopped tomatoes and simmer for 2 minutes. Stir in the tomato purée, red wine and water, season with salt and pepper and bring to the boil.

7. Put the stuffed squid in the sauce, cover with a tight-fitting lid and cook slowly for 45 minutes.

8. Check the seasoning of the sauce and adjust if necessary, then serve.

I've eaten this dish as a starter, main course and, on more than one occasion, as a substantial snack. The rissoles benefit from a long soak in the tomato sauce and in fact I actually prefer them reheated the following day. They will leave you craving for sunshine and ouzo!

Soutzoukákia Smyrneiká

Cumin-spiced Rissoles

 **preparation time**
30
minutes

 **cooking time** about
25
minutes

 **serves**
4 to 6

 *Ingredients*

4 slices of bread	**For the tomato sauce**
500 g (1 lb) minced beef or lamb	2 tablespoons extra virgin olive oil
1 egg, beaten	1 garlic clove, crushed
3 garlic cloves, crushed	250 g (8 oz) tomatoes, skinned, deseeded and finely chopped
2 teaspoons ground cumin	1 tablespoon tomato purée
½ glass of dry white wine	a pinch of sugar
75 g (3 oz) plain flour	2 tablespoons chopped fresh parsley
vegetable oil for shallow-frying	½ glass of dry white wine
salt and freshly ground black pepper	

1 Soak the bread in a little cold water, then squeeze it dry. Put it in a bowl with the minced meat, beaten egg, garlic, cumin and wine. Season with salt and pepper and mix together thoroughly.

2 Mould the mixture into 8 cylindrical shapes. Spread the flour on a plate and coat the rissoles in it.

3 Heat a thin layer of oil in a large frying pan, add the rissoles and cook until golden brown all over.

4 For the sauce, heat the olive oil in a wide pan, add the garlic, chopped tomatoes and tomato purée and cook for 2 minutes.

5 Season with the sugar and some salt and pepper. Stir in the parsley and wine and simmer for 3–5 minutes.

6 Add the rissoles to the pan, turning them over so they are lightly coated with the tomato sauce. Cover and cook gently for 10 minutes and then serve.

Kevin's Tip

In Greece lunch is quite substantial and is generally served fairly late, then followed by a three-hour siesta. I certainly find that a little snooze after a plate of rissoles is a good idea!

I much prefer this dish to the better-known moussaka. It's a satisfyingly savoury mixture of lamb, courgettes, fresh herbs and tomatoes, enriched with red wine, cheese and eggs, then baked with a cheese and breadcrumb crust. Serve with a good green salad.

28

 Meat and Courgette Pie

Sfougáto

 **preparation time** 35 minutes

cooking time 60 to 70 minutes

serves 6

 **Ingredients**

4 tablespoons olive oil

175 g (6 oz) onions, finely chopped

4 garlic cloves, crushed

2 tablespoons chopped fresh dill

1 tablespoon chopped fresh parsley

500 g (1 lb) minced lamb

250 g (8 oz) tomatoes, skinned, deseeded and chopped

1 glass of red wine

150 ml (5 fl oz) chicken or vegetable stock, or water

1 kg (2 lb) courgettes, cut into slices 5 mm (¼ inch) thick

4 eggs

5 tablespoons milk

50 g (2 oz) self-raising flour

125 g (4 oz) cheese, grated (any hard cheese will do)

75 g (3 oz) white breadcrumbs

salt and freshly ground black pepper

1 Preheat the oven to 180°C, 350°F, gas mark 4.

2 Heat the oil in a deep saucepan, add the onions, garlic and herbs and cook gently for 5 minutes. Add the minced lamb and cook, stirring constantly, for about 10 minutes, until well browned. Stir in the tomatoes, red wine and stock or water and season with salt and pepper.

3 Add the courgettes to the pan, cover with a tight-fitting lid and cook gently for 15 minutes or until the courgettes are tender. Remove from the heat and leave to cool slightly.

4 Put the eggs in a large bowl and beat with a whisk until light and fluffy. Add the milk and flour and beat until smooth, then season lightly with salt and pepper.

5 Add the egg mixture to the lamb, together with half the grated cheese, and mix in well.

6 Lightly grease a deep casserole dish and sprinkle half the breadcrumbs over the base.

7 Place the lamb mixture in the casserole. Mix together the remaining cheese and breadcrumbs and sprinkle them over the top. Bake for 30–40 minutes, until the topping is golden brown.

Kevin's Tip

As well as being delicious, this dish freezes very successfully and so it is well worth making an extra amount and storing it for future use.

The subtle blend of apples, mint, honey and cinnamon explodes on the tongue in this stunning pudding. It is lovely served with Greek yoghurt flavoured with retsina and honey but if, like me, you're a traditionalist when it comes to apple puddings, serve with a jug of piping-hot custard.

Karpópitta me Méli

Spiced Fruit Pie

preparation time
30
minutes

cooking time
25
minutes

serves
6

 Ingredients

8 firm eating apples, such as Cox's

juice of 2 lemons

50 g (2 oz) sultanas

50 g (2 oz) dried apricots, chopped

2 ripe bananas, sliced

50 g (2 oz) glacé cherries

2 tablespoons chopped fresh mint

3 tablespoons runny honey

1 teaspoon ground cinnamon

75 g (3 oz) butter, melted

250 g (8 oz) filo pastry

icing sugar for dusting

1 Preheat the oven to 200°C, 400°F, gas mark 6.

2 Quarter and core the apples (but leave the skin on), then slice them thinly and put them into a bowl. Add the lemon juice, sultanas, dried apricots, bananas, glacé cherries and fresh mint. Gently mix the honey through the fruit mixture and then stir in the cinnamon.

3 Grease a deep 17.5 cm (7 inch) flan tin with a little of the melted butter (it's best to use a tin with a removable base).

4 Spread a sheet of filo pastry on a work surface, brush with melted butter, then place in the tin. Repeat with the remaining pastry, ensuring that there is sufficient overlap to cover the top of the pie.

5 Fill with the fruit mixture and bring the overlapping sheets of pastry over the top, crumpling them attractively. Brush the top with the remaining melted butter.

6 Bake for 25 minutes, then remove the sides of the tin and bake for 5 minutes longer, until the pastry is golden brown and crisp. Serve hot or cold, dusted with icing sugar.

Kevin's Tip

Filo pastry can never be made as thinly at home as the commercial version, so this is one of those rare occasions when I would recommend that you use the bought product.

Greece

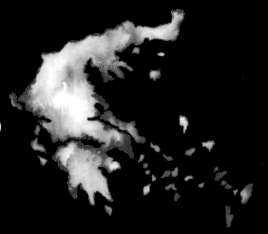

opposite (clockwise from top)

Baked Sardines 16

Stuffed Squid 24

Fried Mussels 14

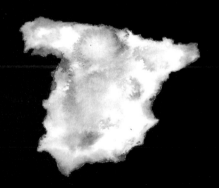

Spain

overleaf (clockwise from top)

Fish Soup 34

Pork Chops with a Pomegranate
Confit 48

Catalan Custard Cream 54

Spain

The Spanish excel at eating 'on the hoof', and have fixed in their culture the famous tapas crawl. This sophisticated version of the pub crawl involves hopping from bar to bar, supping Rioja and snacking on such delicacies as garlic prawns, olives, *patatas bravas* and roast suckling pig. For the tourist, this is a great way to experiment with more adventurous foods. Some of Spain's finest foods are the simplest – hams from Serrano, Asturian bean stews, and the roast vegetables of Gerona, which form part of a deep-rooted tradition of cooking outdoors on open fires. A medley of delights is added to the embers, from peppers, aubergines and baby artichokes to the sweetest of onions, which caramelize a treat. However, Spanish cooks find vegetarianism rather wimpish and tend to 'improve' vegetarian dishes with the addition of a little chicken or beef. Vegans may as well stay at home – unless they're hoping to diet.

Breakfast is typically a social affair. City dwellers go out for their coffee and start the day with bread dipped in oil and topped with Manchego cheese or chorizo sausage. Those with a sweet tooth plump for *churros y chocolate* – doughnuts sprinkled with sugar and served with a cup of hot chocolate. Chocolate is something of a superstar in Spain's rich larder of culinary adoptions. First brought to Spain at the beginning of the 16th century by the *conquistadores* returning from Mexico (where it was cooked up by the Aztecs into an unpalatably bitter brew), cocoa was finally reborn and restyled by the convent nuns of Guajaca into the chocolate drink we know today.

And then there's all that treacle-thick coffee – more fire to add to the fiesta fever that already courses through Spanish veins. Or perhaps it's something in the chorizo that keeps them up all night!

Perhaps the main difference between a Spanish fish soup and one from other Mediterranean countries is the use of bread as a thickening agent.

The result is a full-bodied soup with well-developed flavours. The finish is not as refined as some but the intensity of flavour will excuse that.

Sopa de Pescado
Fish Soup

 **preparation time**
50
minutes

 **cooking time**
35
minutes

 serves
4

 **Ingredients**

250 g (8 oz) leeks, finely shredded

250 g (8 oz) onions, finely shredded

500 g (1 lb) firm white fish on the bone, such as haddock, cod or whiting

1.75 litres (3 pints) cold water

300 ml (10 fl oz) dry white wine

75 ml (3 fl oz) extra virgin olive oil

2 garlic cloves, crushed

2 tablespoons chopped fresh coriander

125 g (4 oz) white bread, crusts removed, diced

1 tablespoon chopped fresh parsley

1 bay leaf

125 g (4 oz) cooked peeled prawns

125 g (4 oz) cooked mussels (see page 15), shelled

175 g (6 oz) cooked clams (see page 43), shelled

500 g (1 lb) tomatoes, skinned, deseeded and diced

1 glass of brandy

salt and freshly ground black pepper

1 Put the leeks, onions, fish, water
and wine in a large pan. Let it rise
slowly to the boil and then simmer
very gently for 20 minutes.

2 Strain through a sieve, reserving
the stock. Remove the flesh from
the bones of the fish and set aside.

3 Heat the oil in a large pan, add
the garlic and coriander and cook
gently for 5 minutes. Stir in the bread
and cook for 2 minutes.

4 Add the parsley, bay leaf, prawns,
mussels and clams and cook for
2 minutes, then stir in the tomatoes,
brandy, reserved fish stock and salt
and pepper.

5 Bring to the boil, then
reduce the heat and add the
cooked white fish. Simmer gently for
5 minutes. Check the seasoning and
adjust if necessary. The consistency of
the soup can be altered by adding a
little more white wine if too thick or a
little more bread if too thin.

6 Serve the soup immediately. You
could float in it some thin slices of
toasted bread that have been smeared
with garlic mayonnaise.

*Most Mediterranean countries claim to produce the best fish soup but in
Britain it is not very popular at all, which is a great shame. This might
be because we consider the preparation to be messy and time-consuming.
Get the fishmonger to prepare the fish for you and you're halfway there.*

These turnovers can be made to any size that takes your fancy and you could use any ingredients for filling them. Small versions called **36** *empanadillas* are often served as tapas in Spain and these, along with a selection of other little delicacies, are all that's needed on a hot afternoon.

Empanadas Valencianas

Leek and Ham Pastries

preparation time
40
minutes

cooking time
30 to *35*
minutes

serves
6

Ingredients

2 tablespoons vegetable oil

175 g (6 oz) leeks, thinly sliced

2 garlic cloves, crushed

3 tomatoes, skinned, deseeded and chopped

125 g (4 oz) cured ham, preferably jamón serrano, diced

2 eggs, hard-boiled and chopped

1 tablespoon chopped fresh basil

1 egg, beaten

salt and freshly ground black pepper

For the pastry

250 g (8 oz) plain flour

½ teaspoon salt

1 tablespoon Ricard (or aniseed-flavoured apéritif)

75 ml (3 fl oz) extra virgin olive oil

1 To make the pastry, sift the flour and salt into a bowl and make a well in the centre. Add the Ricard and olive oil and begin drawing the flour into the liquid. Add just enough cold water to moisten the flour and then work it to a smooth dough. Knead for 2 minutes, then cover with cling film and chill for at least 2 hours.

2 Preheat the oven to 200°C, 400°F, gas mark 6.

3 For the filling, heat the vegetable oil in a saucepan, add the leeks and garlic and cook gently for 5–8 minutes, until softened. Add the tomatoes and cook gently for a further 2 minutes, then stir in the ham and remove from the heat.

4 Add the chopped eggs and basil and season with salt and pepper.

5 Roll the pastry out thinly and cut out 6 (or 12, 24 or 36!) circles. Divide the filling between them, placing it on one half of each circle. Brush a little water around the edge of the pastry, then fold in half to make turnovers. Press the edges together with a fork to seal them and create an attractive finish.

6 Brush the pastries with a little beaten egg to glaze, then transfer them to a lightly greased baking sheet and bake in the preheated oven for about 20–25 minutes, until golden brown. Serve warm.

Kevin's Tip

These are also delightful filled with fresh shellfish, a little garlic and finely chopped fennel or dill. The aniseed flavour of the pastry really enhances the taste of shellfish.

When I'm in Spain, particularly in the Basque region, I often request this dish for a late breakfast or early lunch, depending upon one's perspective. It's like a combination of ratatouille and scrambled eggs and is quite delightful served on hot buttered toast.

Peperrada

Casserole of Peppers in a Tomato and Egg Sauce

preparation time
25
minutes

cooking time about
40
minutes

serves
4

Ingredients

2 red peppers, halved and deseeded

2 green peppers, halved and deseeded

175 ml (6 fl oz) extra virgin olive oil

75 g (3 oz) onions, finely chopped

2 garlic cloves, crushed

1 tablespoon chopped fresh basil

6 tomatoes, skinned, deseeded and chopped

75 g (3 oz) cured ham, preferably jamón serrano, diced

1 bay leaf

4 medium eggs, lightly beaten

salt and freshly ground black pepper

1 Put the peppers skin-side up on a baking tray and brush lightly with a little of the oil. Place under a hot grill until the skin bubbles and blackens. Leave to cool, then peel off the skin and finely slice the peppers.

2 Heat the remaining oil in a saucepan, add the peppers and cook for 5 minutes. Then add the onions and garlic and cook gently, uncovered, for 15 minutes. Stir in the basil and chopped tomatoes and simmer for 5–6 minutes, until the mixture is fairly thick.

3 Add the diced ham and the bay leaf and then season to taste with a little salt and pepper.

4 Slowly pour the beaten eggs into the pan and cook over a gentle heat, stirring constantly, until they are just set.

5 Check the seasoning and adjust if necessary. Serve immediately on hot buttered toast or simply accompanied by a dressed salad.

Kevin's Tip

Roasting and peeling the peppers seems like a time-consuming and tiresome exercise. However, although you can omit this step the finished dish will not have such a good flavour, proving that it is worth the effort in the end.

I first came across this dish in 1996 when I was filming a 'Holiday' report for the BBC on the island of Mallorca. It has to be said that most Mediterranean countries have a way of combining these ingredients as a stand-alone dish but this one is certainly a winner on presentation.

Potato, Aubergine and Tomato Flan

Tumbret

preparation time

50

minutes, plus 30 minutes' salting the aubergines

Ingredients

cooking time

about

50

minutes

serves

4 to 6

2 aubergines, cut into slices 5 mm (¼ inch) thick

2 green peppers, halved and deseeded

2 tablespoons vegetable oil

about 75 ml (3 fl oz) extra virgin olive oil

2 large potatoes, peeled and thinly sliced

4 garlic cloves, crushed

75 g (3 oz) onions, chopped

8 tomatoes, skinned, deseeded and chopped

1 tablespoon tomato purée

2 tablespoons chopped fresh basil

1 tablespoon chopped fresh parsley

1 glass of dry white wine

a pinch of sugar

3 drops of Tabasco sauce

50 g (2 oz) white breadcrumbs

1 tablespoon chopped fresh oregano

salt and freshly ground black pepper

1 Put the aubergines on kitchen paper, sprinkle with salt, and leave for 30 minutes (this will remove any bitterness).

2 Preheat the oven to 200°C, 400°F, gas mark 6. Rinse the aubergines thoroughly under cold running water and pat dry with kitchen paper.

3 Put the peppers skin-side up on a baking tray and brush with the vegetable oil. Put them under a hot grill until the skin bubbles and blackens. Leave to cool, then peel off the skin and slice the peppers.

4 Heat a third of the olive oil in a large frying pan and fry the potato slices until golden brown on both sides. Remove from the pan and set aside.

5 Add half the remaining oil to the pan and fry the aubergine slices for about 2 minutes on each side, until golden brown. You may have to cook them in batches and add more oil to the pan. Arrange the potato and aubergine slices in overlapping layers in a shallow ovenproof dish.

6 Heat the remaining oil in the frying pan, add the garlic and onions and cook gently for 5 minutes, until softened. Stir in the chopped tomatoes, tomato purée, basil, parsley and white wine and cook gently for 5 minutes. Season with the sugar, Tabasco and some salt and pepper.

7 Spread the mixture over the aubergine and potato slices. Mix together the breadcrumbs and chopped oregano and scatter them over the top.

8 Bake for 15 minutes, until the top is browned. Remove from the oven, cover and leave to stand for 5–8 minutes. Place a large plate over the top of the dish and invert to turn out the flan. Serve immediately.

Kevin's Tip

I like to serve this flan with a dish of sliced potatoes that have been fried in a little oil along with sliced onions, crushed garlic and chopped sun-dried tomatoes.

Serving pasta and shellfish together is a wonderful way of combining bulk and flavour. The shellfish willingly passes on an abundance of taste

to the pasta, which is more than happy to absorb it. Any type of pasta will do for this recipe but the bulkier the better.

Pasta with Clams

Fideos con Almejas

preparation time
45
minutes

cooking time
20 to *25*
minutes

serves
4

Ingredients

1.5 kg (3 lb) fresh clams

75 ml (3 fl oz) virgin olive oil

175 g (6 oz) shallots, finely diced

3 garlic cloves, crushed

2 tablespoons chopped fresh dill

500 g (1 lb) tomatoes, skinned, deseeded and diced

300 ml (10 fl oz) dry white wine

350 g (12 oz) dried pasta

150 ml (5 fl oz) crème fraîche

salt and freshly ground black pepper

1 Scrub the clams thoroughly under cold running water, discarding any open ones, then set aside.

2 Heat the oil in a pan, add the shallots, garlic, dill and tomatoes and cook gently for 5–10 minutes. Season with salt and pepper.

3 Pour the white wine into a large shallow pan, bring to the boil and then add the clams. Cover with a lid and cook for a few minutes until the shells open. Discard any that remain closed. Remove the clams from the wine with a slotted spoon and put them in the tomato sauce. Reserve the wine they were cooked in.

4 Pour the reserved wine into a clean large pan, top up with boiling water and, once it comes back to the boil, add the pasta. Season with salt and cook until *al dente*.

5 Drain the pasta well and stir it into the tomato and clam sauce. Check the seasoning and add more salt and pepper if necessary.

6 If the sauce is too thick, add a little more white wine. Once you are satisfied with the consistency, stir in the crème fraîche, heat through briefly and then serve immediately.

Kevin's Tip

The use of crème fraîche gives a lovely light finish to the sauce without making it too creamy. However, if you prefer a sharper flavour to your food then you could leave out the cream.

A visit to Spain would be incomplete without fighting your way through a mountain of paella. It is Spain's finest contribution to the world of gastronomy. Paella often contains chicken, rabbit and even snails but I like this seafood version best of all.

Paella a la Marinera

Seafood Paella

preparation time
40 minutes

cooking time
about **35** minutes

serves
6

Ingredients

18 mussels

75 ml (3 fl oz) extra virgin olive oil

3 garlic cloves, crushed

50 g (2 oz) shallots, finely diced

250 g (8 oz) chicken breasts, skinned and cut into 1 cm (½ inch) dice

1 green pepper, deseeded and thinly sliced

1 red pepper, deseeded and thinly sliced

75 g (3 oz) cured ham, preferably jamón serrano, diced

125 g (4 oz) cleaned squid (see page 25), sliced

50 g (2 oz) stoned black olives

25 g (1 oz) capers, rinsed

350 g (12 oz) tomatoes, skinned, deseeded and sliced

75 g (3 oz) peas

400 g (14 oz) long grain rice

1 glass of dry white wine

4 saffron strands, crushed

1 teaspoon paprika

juice of 1 lemon

1 bay leaf

500 g (1 lb) raw prawns, shelled

fresh coriander leaves, to garnish

salt and freshly ground black pepper

1 Scrub the mussels under cold running water. Pull off the beards and scrape off any barnacles with a small sharp knife. Discard any open mussels that do not close when tapped lightly on a work surface.

2 Heat a little water in a large pan, add the mussels and cover with a tight-fitting lid. Cook over a medium-high heat for 3–5 minutes, until the mussels have opened. Discard any that do not open. Strain the mussels, reserving the cooking liquid. Remove the top shell from each mussel and set the mussels aside.

3 Heat the oil in a paella pan (if you don't have such a thing, all is not lost; simply use a very large frying pan). Add the garlic, shallots and diced chicken, season lightly with salt and pepper and cook for 2–3 minutes, until the chicken is sealed on all sides.

Kevin's Tip

Feel free to alter this recipe to suit your taste. The nice thing about paella is that there are no hard rules about what you can and can't use.

4 Add the sliced peppers, ham and squid and cook for 1 minute, then add the olives, capers, tomatoes and peas. Add the rice and stir well, then pour in the white wine and add the saffron.

5 Top up the mussel cooking liquid with enough water to make 1.2 litres (2 pints) and stir it into the pan. Add the paprika, lemon juice and bay leaf and season well with salt and pepper.

6 Bring to the boil and cook for 10 minutes over a fairly high heat. Reduce the temperature, add the mussels and prawns and cook slowly for 10–12 minutes, until all the stock has been absorbed and the rice is tender.

7 Cover and leave to rest for 5 minutes, which will allow the flavours to develop. Remove the bay leaf, garnish with coriander leaves and serve.

Almonds are plentiful and stunningly good in Spain, and appear in lots of classic recipes there. They are used primarily in sweet dishes but in this savoury recipe they serve two purposes, giving it a subtle underlying flavour and also thickening the sauce.

Chicken in Almond Sauce

Pollo en Pepitoria

preparation time
30
minutes

cooking time
30 to 40
minutes

serves
4

Ingredients

75 ml (3 fl oz) olive oil

1 x 1.6 kg (3½ lb) chicken, cut into 8 pieces

20 whole almonds, skinned, plus 25 g (1 oz) chopped almonds

125 g (4 oz) onions, finely diced

2 garlic cloves, crushed

50 g (2 oz) white bread, crusts removed

a pinch of ground cinnamon

2 tablespoons chopped fresh coriander, plus extra to garnish

150 ml (5 fl oz) dry sherry

300 ml (10 fl oz) chicken stock

a pinch of saffron strands

1 bouquet garni (1 sprig of thyme, 3 sprigs of parsley, 1 bay leaf, all encased in 2 short lengths of celery and tied with string)

75 ml (3 fl oz) double cream

2 egg yolks

25 g (1 oz) sesame seeds, toasted

salt and freshly ground black pepper

1 Heat the oil in a large pan, add the chicken pieces and season on both sides with salt and pepper. Cook over a medium heat until well browned all over, then remove from the pan and set aside.

2 Add the whole almonds to the pan with the onions and garlic and cook gently for 2–3 minutes.

3 Transfer the mixture to a food processor, add the bread, cinnamon and fresh coriander, and blend until smooth. Then mix in the sherry and stock.

4 Put the chicken back in the pan, pour the sauce over and bring slowly to the boil. Add the saffron, bouquet garni and a little salt. Simmer, uncovered, for 20–30 minutes, until the chicken is cooked. If the sauce seems too thick, add a little more stock.

5 Beat together the cream and egg yolks, add a little of the sauce and mix together well, then stir this mixture into the sauce. Heat gently but do not let it boil.

6 Check the seasoning and adjust if necessary. Garnish with the sesame seeds, chopped almonds and some coriander, then serve.

Kevin's Tip

This recipe calls for a lovely savoury rice dish as an accompaniment in order to soak up the sauce. A standard pilaff recipe with the addition of a little tarragon and freshly grated Parmesan works well.

This is a delightful dish to feast one's eyes upon and even nicer to eat. A little extra honey will give a gentler finish, while a dash more balsamic vinegar will sharpen the flavours. Potatoes fried with rosemary and garlic and some creamed spinach make excellent accompaniments.

Chuletas de Cerdo en Salsa de Granadas

Pork Chops
with a Pomegranate Confit

preparation time
20
minutes

cooking time
about
45
minutes

serves
6

*I*ngredients

50 g (2 oz) butter	**For the confit**
4 tablespoons vegetable oil	4 pomegranates
6 pork chops	3 tablespoons runny honey
1 tablespoon paprika	2 tablespoons balsamic vinegar
175 g (6 oz) red onions, thinly sliced	150 ml (5 fl oz) dry white wine
2 garlic cloves, crushed	150 ml (5 fl oz) chicken stock
1 tablespoon chopped fresh oregano	125 g (4 oz) unsalted butter, chilled and diced
salt and freshly ground black pepper	

1 Preheat the oven to 180°C, 350°F, gas mark 4.

2 Heat the butter and vegetable oil in a large frying pan. Dust the pork chops on both sides with the paprika, season with salt and pepper and add to the pan. Cook for about 4–5 minutes on each side, until well browned, then remove from the pan and place in a casserole dish.

3 Add the sliced onions, garlic and oregano to the frying pan and cook gently until soft. Place them on top of the chops, then transfer to the oven and bake for 15–20 minutes, until the chops are cooked through.

4 To make the confit, halve the pomegranates and scoop out the seeds, leaving behind the bitter membranes. Pour off surplus fat from the frying pan, add the pomegranate seeds, honey and balsamic vinegar and simmer for 4–5 minutes. Pour in the white wine and boil until reduced in volume by a third. Add the stock and bring to the boil.

5 Draw the pan off the heat and whisk the unsalted butter into the sauce a few pieces at a time. Season with salt and pepper and serve with the chops.

Kevin's Tip

A much underused fruit, the pomegranate grows throughout the Mediterranean and as far east as India. Providing you discard the bitter membranes, it is versatile enough to use in all forms of cooking.

A hearty dish of Valencian origins. Each ingredient plays its part in maximizing flavour. The chickpeas add body and texture, the *pelota* (meatball) is a tasty and intriguing addition, while the inclusion of white and black pudding seems excessive but really makes a difference.

50

Arroz Rosetxat

*L*amb and Rice Casserole

Ingredients

preparation time
45
minutes, plus soaking the chickpeas overnight

cooking time
about
2 1/2
hours

serves
6 to *8*

250 g (8 oz) boned lamb, cut into chunks

2.75 litres (5 pints) cold water

75 g (3 oz) carrots, finely chopped

50 g (2 oz) onion, finely chopped

75 g (3 oz) celery, finely chopped

125 g (4 oz) turnips, finely chopped

5 garlic cloves, crushed

150 g (5 oz) chickpeas, soaked in cold water for 24 hours, then drained

1 bay leaf

1 bouquet garni (1 sprig of thyme, 3 sprigs of parsley, 1 bay leaf, all encased in 2 short lengths of celery and tied with string)

125 g (4 oz) black pudding, sliced

125 g (4 oz) white pudding, sliced

4 tablespoons olive oil

300 g (10 oz) long grain rice

4 saffron strands

salt and freshly ground black pepper

For the meatball

2 slices of white bread, toasted

175 g (6 oz) minced pork

2 garlic cloves, crushed

1 egg, lightly beaten

a pinch of allspice

50 g (2 oz) pine nuts

1 tablespoon chopped fresh parsley

1 Put the lamb in a large pan with the water, bring to the boil and then drain off the water. Add the same amount of cold water as before, bring to the boil and reduce the heat to a simmer.

2 Add the vegetables, 3 cloves of the garlic, the chickpeas, bay leaf and bouquet garni and simmer very gently for 45 minutes. Then add the black and white puddings and continue cooking for 10 minutes. Season with salt and pepper.

3 To make the meatball, put the toasted bread in a food processor and process to crumbs. Add the minced pork, garlic, egg, allspice, pine nuts and parsley. Season with salt and pepper and process briefly to combine. Remove and shape into a large ball.

4 Add the meatball to the lamb and simmer for about an hour, until the meatball is cooked and the chickpeas are tender. Carefully strain off the stock and set aside.

5 Preheat the oven to 180°C, 350°F, gas mark 4.

6 Heat the olive oil in a pan, add the remaining garlic and the rice and cook without colouring for 2 minutes. Add the saffron, moisten with a little of the stock and then add the lamb, chickpeas and vegetables (but not the meatball). Gently stir in about 900 ml (1½ pints) of the stock.

7 Transfer the mixture to an ovenproof casserole dish. Slice the meatball and lay the slices on top. Cover and bake for about 15–20 minutes, until the rice is tender.

Kevin's Tip

This dish originally would have been designed to make use of cooked meat left over from a previous meal and can be adapted accordingly.

The literal translation of this recipe title is 'puffs of air'. These delightfully light and fluffy little doughnuts will readily play host to any filling that takes your fancy. On a very hot day you could even try squeezing a little ice cream inside them.

Buñuelos de Viento

*L*emon Custard Puffs

preparation time
40
minutes

cooking time
about
25
minutes

serves
6

*I*ngredients

125 ml (4 fl oz) milk	vegetable oil for deep-frying
125 ml (4 fl oz) water	a pinch of allspice
40 g (1½ oz) butter	**For the filling**
40 g (1½ oz) caster sugar, plus extra for coating	3 eggs
a pinch of salt	150 g (5 oz) caster sugar
2 tablespoons brandy	150 g (5 oz) plain flour
finely grated zest of 1 lemon	750 ml (1¼ pints) milk
75 g (3 oz) plain flour	1 vanilla pod
2 eggs	finely grated zest of 1 lemon
1 egg white	40 g (1½ oz) butter

*K*evin's Tip

This is a failsafe recipe provided you heed the warning in step 6 regarding the incorporation of the flour paste into the eggs and egg white.

1 First make the filling. Lightly whisk together the eggs and sugar, then gradually whisk in the flour and add just a little of the milk. Bring the remaining milk to the boil with the vanilla pod.

2 Remove the vanilla pod from the milk, then add the lemon zest and gradually pour the milk on to the egg mixture, whisking constantly until smooth.

3 Return the mixture to the pan and stir over a low heat for 3–5 minutes until it thickens. Stir in the butter. Remove from the heat, cover with cling film and leave to cool.

4 To make the batter for the doughnuts, put the milk and water in a saucepan with the butter, sugar, salt, brandy and lemon zest. Bring slowly to the boil and then remove from the heat.

5 Rain in the flour, beating vigorously. Place the pan back on a low heat and continue beating until the mixture forms a ball. Set aside to cool slightly.

6 Lightly whisk together the eggs and egg white and then gradually whisk in the flour paste. Be careful not to add it too quickly or the mixture will curdle.

7 Using 2 dessertspoons that have been warmed in hot water, shape scoops of dough into ovals, turning it between the spoons to make a smooth shape.

8 Heat the vegetable oil in a deep saucepan and cook the doughnuts a few at a time for 4–5 minutes, until golden brown. (You will need to turn them over carefully during cooking as they will double in size.) Remove from the oil with a slotted spoon and drain on kitchen paper.

9 When the puffs are cold, put the filling into a piping bag with a small plain nozzle and fill the puffs by injecting the nozzle through them. Mix the allspice with a little caster sugar and roll the doughnuts in it.

Without doubt the nicest pudding to come out of Spain, this is a great dessert for dinner parties. The custard can be made in advance and the sugar topping added just before serving. If your figure and constitution can stand it, substitute double cream for the milk. I know my figure can't!

Crema Catalana

Catalan Custard Cream

preparation time
15
minutes, plus chilling time

cooking time
10
minutes

serves
4

Ingredients

125 g (4 oz) caster sugar

3 egg yolks

1½ teaspoons cornflour

350 ml (12 fl oz) milk

finely grated zest of ½ lemon

a pinch of ground cinnamon

1 Whisk 75 g (3 oz) of the caster sugar with the egg yolks until very pale and thick – the mixture should be thick enough to leave a trail on the surface for a few seconds when drizzled from the whisk.

2 Dissolve the cornflour in 1 tablespoon of the milk. Put the rest of the milk in a saucepan with the grated lemon zest and cinnamon and bring to the boil.

3 Pour a little of the hot milk on to the egg mixture and whisk it in. Gradually add the rest of the milk, whisking constantly, and then return it to the pan. Add the dissolved cornflour and stir constantly over a low heat until the custard has thickened, taking care not to overcook the mixture.

4 Strain the custard into a large jug. Pour it into ramekin dishes and leave to cool, then chill.

5 Sprinkle the remaining caster sugar over the puddings in an even layer and place them under a hot grill until golden brown. Serve with either a small bowl of soft fruit or *langues de chat* biscuits.

Kevin's Tip

If you follow the recipe carefully the custard shouldn't curdle. However, if it does, then quickly remove the custard from the heat and whisk in a little ice-cold water.

In this recipe every bit of flavour is drawn from the bananas by roasting them in their skins before adding them to the cake mixture. I hate to admit it but I like to have this cake with custard and ice cream. It's no wonder I'm getting fat!

Torta de Platanos

Banana Cake

preparation time

45

minutes

cooking time

40 to 45

minutes

serves

6

(but not in our house!)

Ingredients

2 firm but ripe bananas

125 g (4 oz) butter

250 g (8 oz) caster sugar

4 eggs, beaten

125 g (4 oz) plain flour

2 teaspoons baking powder

1 teaspoon ground cinnamon

½ teaspoon freshly grated nutmeg

a pinch of allspice

75 g (3 oz) ground almonds

75 g (3 oz) raisins

1 Preheat the oven to 200°C, 400°F, gas mark 6.

2 Bake the bananas in their skins for about 5–6 minutes, then remove from the oven and leave to cool. Reduce the oven temperature to 180°C, 350°F, gas mark 4.

3 Cream the butter and sugar together until pale and fluffy. Beat in the eggs a little at a time.

4 Peel the bananas and then mash the flesh to a purée. Stir the purée into the cake mixture.

5 Sift the flour with the baking powder and spices and, using a metal spoon, fold it gently into the cake mixture. Finally fold in the ground almonds and raisins.

6 Transfer the mixture to a lightly greased and floured 20 x 30 cm (8 x 12 inch) baking tin, spreading it evenly. Bake for about 35–40 minutes, until well risen and golden brown. Leave to cool on a wire rack.

Kevin's Tip

This cake will keep in an airtight container for 3–4 days or longer in the freezer. Some people actually consider that the cake improves with age (not like me).

Spain

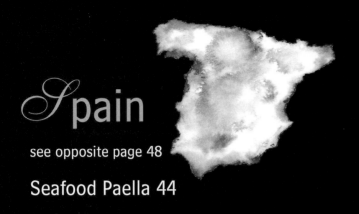

see opposite page 48

Seafood Paella 44

Italy

see opposite page 49 (clockwise from top)

Tiramisù 77

Chicken with Tarragon 70

Flatbreads with Spinach 62

Italy

The jewel in the crown of Italian cooking is pasta. Forget the dried stuff in packets, the finest pasta I've ever tasted is the fresh variety prepared in Naples. Apparently this level of excellence is down to the quality of the water, which is said to be chemically superior to that anywhere else in Italy. Or maybe they're just better cooks.

It was the Neapolitans, too, who masterminded the pizza. The Americans can only claim the credit for the great PR job they've done for the takeaway. The inventive Neapolitans were also the first people to freeze cream in order to make a sweet that you can truly stick your tongue in when you lick it from a cone.

Anyone who tells you that eating a whole load of food with the same flavour is boring has misread the Italian menu. This common mistake occurs when pasta is ordered as a main course. There is an infinite variety of Italian main courses, ranging from beautifully cooked poultry with herbs, meats simmered in wine, and seafood dishes that have won world acclaim.

The historic split between North and South plays a powerful part in dividing up the diet. The North has always been closer both geographically and in spirit to Germany and France. Risotto is the North's secret weapon but, often presented as a grey, gloomy mass in a bowl, it is not an easy dish for the British to get their teeth into. Don't be fooled by its appearance. The use of fine vegetables and spices and prized Arborio rice turns this dish into one for which it is worth acquiring the taste.

Much to the delight of my tastebuds, Italy has managed to cling on to its ancient regional identities and is fiercely traditional when it comes to food – almost to the point of culinary chauvinism. To the Italians 'tasting foreign exotica' means sampling a dish from the neighbouring town!

This recipe produces a hearty soup which, when served with warm focaccia bread, makes a meal in itself, perfect for a cold winter day.

Zuppa di Fagioli

Bean Soup

preparation time

15

minutes, plus 24 hours
soaking the beans

cooking time
about

1 to *1¾*
hours

serves

6

1 Heat the oil in a deep pan, add the onions and garlic and cook gently for 10 minutes, until tender.

2 Add the stock and bring to the boil, then add all the rest of the ingredients except the parsley, basil and seasoning. Simmer gently until the beans are tender – this can take anything from 45 minutes–1½ hours, depending on the age of the beans.

3 Season well with salt and pepper, stir in the parsley and basil and then serve.

Ingredients

1 tablespoon olive oil

75 g (3 oz) onions, finely chopped

2 garlic cloves, crushed

1.2 litres (2 pints) vegetable or chicken stock

250 g (8 oz) dried cannellini beans, soaked in cold water for 24 hours, then drained

125 g (4 oz) celery, finely chopped

75 g (3 oz) carrots, finely chopped

50 g (2 oz) leeks, finely chopped

3 medium potatoes, chopped

4 tomatoes, skinned, deseeded and chopped

75 g (3 oz) sugarsnap peas, chopped

1 bay leaf

1 tablespoon chopped fresh parsley

1 tablespoon chopped fresh basil

salt and freshly ground black pepper

The mascarpone in this recipe gives the crostini a creamy lightness, allowing the flavour of the smoked salmon to be savoured to the full.

Crostini con Salmone Affumicato
Crostini with Smoked Salmon

preparation time 5 minutes

cooking time 5 minutes

serves 4

Ingredients

125 g (4 oz) mascarpone cheese

75 g (3 oz) smoked salmon, finely diced

juice of ¼ lemon

1 tablespoon chopped fresh dill

a pinch of cayenne pepper

4 slices of good-quality bread
(the firmer the better)

1 tablespoon paprika

freshly ground black pepper

1 Mix together the mascarpone cheese, smoked salmon, lemon juice, dill and cayenne pepper, adding freshly ground black pepper to taste.

2 Toast the slices of bread on a ridged cast-iron grill pan or fry in a little olive oil until golden on both sides.

3 Spread the mascarpone and salmon mixture evenly on the toasted bread and then heat under a grill just until the topping bubbles.

4 Lightly dust the crostini with the paprika and then serve straight away.

Piadina, a rustic hearthbread from Romagna, is centuries old and used to be baked on stones set over an open fire. It is traditionally served warm

with sautéed greens or other toppings such as prosciutto or cheese. Fresh *piadine* and a glass of chilled Frascati make the perfect snack.

Flatbreads with Spinach

Piadine con Spinaci

preparation time
50
minutes, plus 1 hour for the dough to rest

cooking time about
40
minutes

serves
6

Ingredients

600 g (1¼ lb) plain flour

25 g (1 oz) butter, softened

900 g (2 lb) fresh spinach, washed

2 tablespoons extra virgin olive oil

2 garlic cloves, chopped

75 g (3 oz) onions, finely chopped

¼ teaspoon freshly grated nutmeg

50 g (2 oz) pine nuts, toasted

25 g (1 oz) raisins

75 g (3 oz) ricotta cheese

75 g (3 oz) fresh Parmesan cheese, grated

salt and freshly ground black pepper

1 Sift the flour into a large bowl with a pinch of salt. Add the softened butter and enough warm water to make a firm dough. Turn the dough out on to a work surface and knead for 15 minutes, until smooth and elastic, then cover with a damp cloth and leave to rest for 1 hour.

2 Divide the dough into pieces about the size of a pingpong ball and flatten them with the palm of your hand to 5 mm (¼inch) thick.

3 Heat a dry heavy-based frying pan or a cast-iron griddle until very hot, then cook the *piadine* in it for 4–5 minutes, until they are slightly burnt underneath and bubbles appear on the surface. Turn over and cook the other side, then remove from the pan and cover them to keep warm.

4 Place the spinach in a deep pan with just the water clinging to its leaves, cover and cook for a few minutes until wilted and tender. Drain well, squeezing out excess moisture, and chop finely.

5 Heat the oil in a pan, add the garlic and onions and cook until soft. Add the chopped spinach, nutmeg, pine nuts and raisins and mix until the spinach is heated through.

6 Stir in the ricotta and Parmesan and season with salt and pepper. Pile neatly on to the warm breads and serve straight away.

Kevin's Tip

Try serving the topping for these breads on its own or as an accompaniment. It has become a favourite way of serving spinach in our house.

Do use risotto rice such as Arborio for this dish as it gives the best results. Arborio rice is available from most supermarkets now, while other varieties, such as Carnaroli and Vialone Nano, can be found in some large supermarkets and in Italian delicatessens.

Risotto al Pomodoro e Basilica

Tomato and Basil Risotto

preparation time

20

minutes

cooking time

30

minutes

serves

6

Ingredients

1 tablespoon extra virgin olive oil

125 g (4 oz) shallots, finely chopped

1 garlic clove, crushed

500 ml (18 fl oz) vegetable or chicken stock

350 g (12 oz) Arborio rice

12 ripe tomatoes, skinned, deseeded and sliced

50 g (2 oz) unsalted butter

50 g (2 oz) fresh Parmesan cheese, grated

2 tablespoons fresh basil leaves, torn into small pieces

salt and freshly ground black pepper

1 Heat the olive oil in a deep saucepan, add the shallots and garlic and cook gently for a few minutes, until softened but not coloured. Meanwhile, heat the stock to simmering point in a separate pan.

2 Add the rice to the shallots and garlic and cook for 4 minutes, stirring frequently, until the rice is glistening. Stir in the tomatoes, followed by a ladleful of the hot stock.

3 Season lightly with salt and pepper and stir until the stock has been absorbed. The mixture should just be bubbling.

4 Add another ladleful of stock and stir until that too has been absorbed. Keep adding the stock in this way until it has all been absorbed and the rice is tender but still slightly *al dente* – this will take about 20 minutes. If all your stock is used up before the rice is ready, add some hot water.

5 Using a fork, mix in the butter, Parmesan cheese and torn basil leaves. Check the seasoning and adjust if necessary. Serve immediately.

The secret of making perfect risotto is simple: patience and attention to detail. The stock used should be pure and flavour-packed and it should be added gradually, giving time for the rice to absorb it while cooking gently. The rice needs to be simmered very slowly and stirred frequently. Both butter and Parmesan should only be added once the risotto is fully cooked, just before it is served.

This dish of courgettes stuffed with a light cheesy filling and then baked in a tomato sauce can be served as a starter, a snack or an accompaniment to a main course. It also has the advantage of being ideal to make in advance, chill and then reheat when required.

Zucchine alla Parmigiana

Courgettes Stuffed with Ricotta, Basil and Parmesan

preparation time
30
minutes

cooking time
20 to *25*
minutes

serves *8*
as a starter
or accompaniment, *4*
as a main course

Ingredients

2 tablespoons extra virgin olive oil

8 tomatoes, skinned, deseeded and chopped

2 garlic cloves, chopped

250 g (8 oz) ricotta cheese

25 g (1 oz) fresh basil, chopped

1 teaspoon freshly grated nutmeg

75 g (3 oz) fresh Parmesan cheese, grated

2 egg yolks

8 large courgettes

salt and freshly ground black pepper

1 Preheat the oven to 190°C, 375°F, gas mark 5.

2 Heat the olive oil in a saucepan, add the tomatoes and garlic and cook for a few minutes until the mixture has gained body. Season with salt and pepper to taste and then remove from the heat.

3 Mix the ricotta cheese, basil, nutmeg, Parmesan and egg yolks together in a bowl until they form a firm paste and then season well with salt and pepper.

4 Cut the courgettes in half lengthways and scoop out the flesh. Chop the flesh finely and stir into the ricotta and Parmesan cheese mixture. Fill the courgette shells with this mixture and place them in an ovenproof serving dish.

5 Pour the tomato mixture around the stuffed courgettes and bake, uncovered, for 15–18 minutes, until the courgettes are tender and the filling is golden brown.

Kevin's Tip

The filling in this recipe can also be used for stuffing courgette flowers, if you grow your own courgettes or manage to obtain the flowers at a specialist greengrocer's. For a slightly more adventurous finish, try using a mild, blue-veined Italian cheese, such as dolcelatte.

This makes a hearty and satisfying vegetarian main course. Fried aubergines are layered with spinach and courgettes, then covered with a

rich cheese and chive sauce and baked in the oven. Serve with a lightly dressed green salad, warm crusty bread and a large glass of Barolo.

Melanzane al Forno

Aubergine, Spinach and Courgette Casserole

 **preparation time**
50
minutes, plus **30 minutes'** salting the aubergines

 **cooking time**
60 to 70
minutes

 serves
4

Ingredients

3 aubergines, thinly sliced	40 g (1½ oz) butter
125 ml (4 fl oz) olive oil	40 g (1½ oz) plain flour
175 g (6 oz) onions, finely chopped	450 ml (15 fl oz) milk
3 garlic cloves, crushed	75 g (3 oz) fresh Parmesan cheese, grated
750 g (1½ lb) fresh spinach, washed	1 egg yolk
a pinch of freshly grated nutmeg	3 tablespoons chopped fresh chives
250 g (8 oz) courgettes, peeled and thinly sliced	salt and freshly ground black pepper

1 Put the aubergine slices on kitchen paper, sprinkle with salt and leave for 30 minutes.

2 Preheat the oven to 180°C, 350°F, gas mark 4. Drain off the liquid from the aubergines and rinse under cold running water, then pat the aubergines dry with kitchen paper.

3 Heat half the oil in a large frying pan, add the aubergine slices (you will probably have to cook them in batches) and cook briefly on both sides until lightly browned. Remove from the pan and set aside.

4 Heat the remaining oil in the pan, add the onions and garlic and cook gently for 5 minutes, until softened but not coloured. Add the spinach, season with salt, pepper and the nutmeg and cook for 2 minutes, until wilted. Drain off any liquid.

5 Lightly grease a casserole dish. Arrange a third of the aubergine slices in it, top with half the spinach and then half the courgettes. Repeat these layers once more and finish with a layer of aubergine.

6 Melt the butter in a pan, add the flour and cook over a gentle heat until it has a sandy texture. Slowly whisk in the milk and bring the sauce to the boil. Cook gently for 1 minute, then remove from the heat.

7 Stir the grated Parmesan, egg yolk and chives into the sauce and season to taste with salt and pepper.

8 Pour the sauce over the vegetables and bake for 25–30 minutes, until bubbling and golden brown.

Kevin's Tip

It's well worth devoting a little time and effort to salting and rinsing the aubergines before frying them. This will ensure that the flesh remains firm and free from any bitterness.

The subtle flavours of tarragon and lemon blend beautifully in this Sicilian recipe, especially when it is served with olive-oil-mashed potatoes or freshly made pasta (see page 76), along with a glass of lightly chilled Chianti. All that's missing is some glorious sunshine.

Stufato di Pollo e Targone

Chicken with Tarragon

 **preparation time** 35 minutes

 **cooking time** about 2 hours

 serves 4

 **Ingredients**

1 x 1.5 kg (3 lb) chicken	1 small glass of marsala or sherry
125 g (4 oz) onions, finely diced	125 g (4 oz) button onions, peeled
125 g (4 oz) celery, finely diced	125 g (4 oz) button mushrooms, peeled
50 g (2 oz) leek, finely diced	125 ml (4 fl oz) double cream
50 g (2 oz) carrot, finely diced	2 egg yolks
1 bay leaf	a pinch of paprika
1 bouquet garni (1 sprig of thyme, 3 sprigs of parsley, 1 bay leaf, all encased in 2 short lengths of celery and tied with string)	juice of 1 lemon
	2 tablespoons chopped fresh tarragon
50 g (2 oz) butter	salt and freshly ground black pepper
50 g (2 oz) plain flour	

1 Rinse the chicken thoroughly and put it in a large pan. Cover with cold water, bring to the boil and then drain.

2 Top up with fresh cold water to cover, add the chopped vegetables, bay leaf, bouquet garni and some salt and pepper, then bring to the boil. Cover with a tight-fitting lid and simmer gently for 1½ hours or until the chicken is cooked. Remove the chicken from the stock and set aside.

3 Melt the butter in a clean pan, add the flour and stir over a gentle heat for a few minutes. Gradually strain on a little of the chicken stock and mix with a wooden spoon. Continue to add the stock until the sauce has a coating consistency. Pour in the marsala or sherry and add the button onions. Cook gently for 5 minutes.

4 Remove the skin from the chicken and cut the bird into 8 pieces, discarding the carcass. Put the chicken pieces in the sauce and add the mushrooms.

5 Mix the cream with the egg yolks. Pour a little of the hot sauce on to this mixture and stir until well blended, then pour the mixture into the sauce. Mix gently but thoroughly over a low heat.

6 Season with the paprika, lemon juice and some salt and pepper, then add the tarragon. Do not let the mixture boil but simmer very gently for 5 minutes to allow the tarragon to infuse. Serve immediately.

Kevin's Tip

It is possible to adapt this recipe in order to use leftover roast chicken from a previous meal. Simply begin at step 3, using ready-prepared stock, which is available in all good supermarkets, or making your own from the chicken carcass.

Braciole is used to describe a piece of meat without any bones, and this invariably involves the meat being stuffed, rolled and then tied with string before long, slow cooking. Here, beef is rolled up with prosciutto, then cooked in a rich tomato, red wine and mushroom sauce.

Braciole

Stuffed Beef Braised with Prosciutto

preparation time
25
minutes, plus 2 hours' soaking time for the mushrooms

cooking time
about
2 ¹⁄₂
hours

serves
4

Ingredients

350 g (12 oz) topside of beef

125 g (4 oz) prosciutto, thinly sliced

2 tablespoons chopped fresh fennel herb

2 tablespoons torn fresh basil leaves

3 tablespoons olive oil

2 garlic cloves, crushed

125 g (4 oz) onions, finely chopped

50 g (2 oz) dried porcini mushrooms, soaked in hot water for 2 hours, then drained

225 g (8 oz) tomatoes, skinned, deseeded and diced

150 ml (5 fl oz) heavy red wine

salt and freshly ground black pepper

1 Preheat the oven to 190°C, 375°F, gas mark 5.

2 Slice the beef into 8 steaks. Place between 2 sheets of cling film and flatten gently with a rolling pin or meat mallet until they are very thin.

3 Cover each piece with the prosciutto and top with the fennel and basil. Season lightly with salt and pepper. Roll up each piece carefully and secure with string or cocktail sticks.

4 Heat the oil in a wide, heavy-based casserole. Add the beef rolls and cook until browned on all sides. Remove from the casserole and leave to one side.

5 Add the garlic and onions to the casserole and cook gently until soft but not browned. Then add the porcini and tomatoes. Mix together and cook for 2 minutes, then pour in the wine. Season with salt and pepper.

6 Immerse the beef rolls in the sauce. Bring to a simmer, then cover with a tight-fitting lid and transfer to the oven. Cook for 2 hours, until the meat is tender.

7 Remove the string or cocktail sticks from the beef and serve with the sauce.

Kevin's Tip

You can experiment with the filling for these beef rolls. Try using different herbs, or adding thin slices of fontina cheese.

Veal is probably one of the most popular meats served in Italy and recipes for it are legion. If you have any difficulty getting hold of veal, or

perhaps would prefer not to eat it, then this recipe also works perfectly well with pork fillet.

Vitello alla Mozzarella

Veal Escalopes with Mozzarella

preparation time
20
minutes

cooking time about
20
minutes

serves
6

Ingredients

6 veal escalopes, weighing about 750 g (1½ lb) in total	1 small glass of sherry
2 tablespoons olive oil	1 small glass of dry white wine
50 g (2 oz) butter	300 ml (10 fl oz) double cream
75 g (3 oz) shallots, finely chopped	50 g (2 oz) mozzarella cheese, diced
1 garlic clove, crushed	finely grated zest and juice of ½ lemon
75 g (3 oz) wild mushrooms, sliced	a pinch of paprika
75 g (3 oz) leeks, shredded	6 sprigs of fresh sage
1 tablespoon chopped fresh sage	salt and freshly ground black pepper

1 Place each veal escalope between 2 sheets of cling film and flatten gently with a rolling pin or meat mallet until very thin. Season the meat on both sides with salt and pepper.

2 Heat the oil in a large frying pan, add the butter and, once melted, add the escalopes (in batches if necessary). Cook for 1–2 minutes on each side, until browned, then remove from the pan and keep warm.

3 Add the shallots to the pan and fry for 1 minute. Stir in the garlic, wild mushrooms and leeks and cook for 4 minutes, until softened. Add the chopped sage, sherry and white wine and boil until the liquid has reduced by a third.

4 Pour in the double cream and bring to the boil, then turn down the heat and add the mozzarella. Stir until the cheese has melted into the sauce.

5 Add the lemon zest and juice and the paprika, then season with salt and pepper. If the sauce seems too thick, add a little more white wine or sherry until it is to your liking.

6 Put the escalopes on warm serving plates and pour the sauce around. Garnish each one with a sprig of sage and then serve.

Kevin's Tip

Before you flatten the veal escalopes, be sure to remove the wide strip of sinew covering the surface of each one – or ask your butcher to do this for you. Be careful when flattening them that you do not bash them too enthusiastically and make holes in the meat.

It's so easy to produce fresh pasta and, once made, it can either be cook
immediately or stored in a plastic bag in the fridge for 4–5 days.

76

Pasta Fresca
Fresh Pasta

Ingredients

500 g (1 lb) plain flour,
preferably Italian '00' flour

½ teaspoon salt

4 medium eggs

2 teaspoons olive oil

preparation time
about
45
minutes, plus 20-30
minutes to rest
the dough

cooking time
1 to *2*
minutes

serves *6*

1 Sift the flour and salt together on to a
work surface and make a well in the
centre. Add the eggs and olive oil to the well
and gradually mix in the flour to form a
smooth dough. If the dough feels very dry,
then add a few drops of cold water to make it
pliable. (If you have a food processor, simply
blend all the ingredients together in it until
they form a dough.)

2 Knead the dough very firmly on a
lightly floured work surface for about
10 minutes, until it feels smooth and elastic.
Cover with cling film and leave to rest for
20–30 minutes.

3 If you have a pasta machine, use to roll
out the dough. If not, divide it into 4 and
roll out each portion as thinly as possible with
a rolling pin; it should be almost transparent.

4 Cut the dough into ribbons (as thick or
as thin as you like), then leave them for
about 10 minutes to dry slightly.

5 Either coil up the ribbons, cover and
store in the fridge, or cook them in a
large pan of boiling salted water for
1–2 minutes until *al dente*, drain and serve
straight away, with the sauce of your choice.

A holiday in Italy wouldn't be complete without a heaped serving of this 'pick-me-up pudding', yet the recipe is only about 20 years old.

Tiramisù

preparation time
30
minutes, plus
chilling overnight

serves
6

1 Whisk the egg yolks and caster sugar together until pale and creamy; the mixture should be thick enough to leave a trail on the surface when drizzled from the whisk. Fold in the mascarpone cheese.

2 Mix the coffee with the brandy and rum and dip the biscuits into it just to moisten them.

3 Cover the base of a serving dish with a layer of soaked biscuits and then spread some of the mascarpone mixture on top. Sprinkle with some grated chocolate. Repeat these layers until all the ingredients have been used.

4 Chill the tiramisù overnight and then decorate with the nuts before serving.

Ingredients

4 egg yolks

50 g (2 oz) caster sugar

175 g (6 oz) mascarpone cheese

300 ml (10 fl oz) freshly made black coffee

4 tablespoons brandy

2 tablespoons rum

36 boudoir biscuits

125 g (4 oz) good-quality plain chocolate, grated

3 tablespoons chopped mixed nuts

For me, the mere aroma of Amaretto liqueur provokes happy memories of the Italian Riviera, and this is my favourite pudding for a hot sunny day. Although I have to confess that the best I ever tasted was in a scruffy little café near the beach on market day in Ventimiglia.

Souffle di Amaretto Gelato

Amaretto Parfait

preparation time

45

minutes

serves

6

Ingredients

125 g (4 oz) amaretti biscuits

1 small glass of Amaretto liqueur

1 lemon

1 tablespoon powdered gelatine

6 eggs, separated

175 g (6 oz) soft brown sugar

450 ml (15 fl oz) double cream, lightly whipped

25 g (1 oz) cocoa powder

1 Break the biscuits into pieces and place them in a bowl. Pour over the liqueur and leave to soak.

2 Grate the zest from the lemon into a bowl and squeeze the juice over the zest. Stir in the gelatine, then put the bowl over a pan of very hot water, making sure the water does not touch the base of the bowl. Leave until the gelatine has dissolved.

3 Whisk the egg yolks and sugar in a bowl until pale and thick – the mixture should leave a trail on the surface when drizzled from the whisk.

4 Using a metal spoon, fold in the biscuits, followed by the gelatine mixture and then the whipped cream. Be sure to mix in all the ingredients lightly but thoroughly.

5 Whisk the egg whites until they form soft peaks and then fold them carefully into the mixture.

6 Fix a paper or foil collar around a 900 ml (1½ pint) soufflé dish (or 6 ramekins) so that it extends about 5 cm (2 inches) above the rim, securing the collar with sticky tape or paper clips. Transfer the soufflé mixture to the dish and place it in the freezer for at least 24 hours. Remove the collar and dust the surface of the parfait with the cocoa powder before serving.

Kevin's Reflection

I'm forever amazed when crossing into one country from another at the whole concept of borders and boundaries. Never more so than when going from the sophistication of Monte Carlo and elegance of Menton in the South of France to Ventimiglia in Italy. You know without a doubt that you have arrived – lines of washing everywhere and great pasta!

Italy

opposite

Tomato and Basil Risotto 64

France

overleaf (clockwise from top)

Casserole of Wild Mushrooms 88

Grilled Goat's Cheese and
Polenta Salad 84

Country Pâté 86

France

When I say I stand in praise of the French tart do not be dismayed. I am, of course, referring to those perfect pastry cases that thrill in an entirely innocent way. French tarts are about as good as they come – leek lovers plump for the *flamiche* of Picardy, while potato-holics head for Alsace and their *tarte aux vigneronnes*. My personal favourite is the *tarte à l'oignon*, smothered with perfectly caramelized onions.

Although French cooking seems very meat based, vegetables were, in fact, an important part of the diet right up to the end of the 19th century and many splendid regional vegetable dishes still remain. Think of the *garbure* of the Pyrénées, a thick soup of cabbage, peppers, potatoes and haricot beans, and the *potage* of Lorraine, a comforting broth of potatoes and leeks.

French tastes may seem quirky to the British: they like to eat their meat rare, their vegetables *al dente* and their crème caramel blowtorched to a crisp. Alcohol is an essential part of French cooking. If it's not in the dish then it's served with it, and quite often it will be both. In Normandy the alcohol of choice is cider and in Flanders beer, while wine reigns in the rest of the country. The excesses of traditional French cooking do not stop at booze – butter, crème fraîche and eggs enrich dishes from *sole à la normande* to *tarte Tatin*. What can you do but roll home and diet?

Don't be fooled, however, into believing that rich, fancy and elaborate always means good. Like the *couture*, the cuisine of France depends on clean lines, a perfect cut and good materials to work with. The success of many dishes relies on meticulous simplicity. Go to any rural auberge and savour the delights of a simple vegetable soup or home-farm chicken grilled with tarragon. French food is not nearly as pretentious as you may have once believed.

A delightful dish to serve as a starter or an accompaniment. If you are able to get hold of courgette flowers – perhaps if you grow them in your garden – then prepare yourself for a very special treat. They can be cooked in the same way and are even nicer.

Beignets de Courgettes au Parmesan

Courgette Fritters
with Parmesan Cheese

preparation time

20
minutes, plus 2
hours' chilling

cooking time
about
15
minutes

serves
6

Ingredients

40 g (1½ oz) butter

50 g (2 oz) fresh Parmesan cheese, grated

175 g (6 oz) plain flour

1 teaspoon fine salt

250 ml (8 fl oz) light ale

2 egg whites

vegetable oil for deep-frying

750 g (1½ lb) firm courgettes, cut into slices
5 mm (¼ inch) thick

1 Melt the butter gently and then stir in the Parmesan cheese.

2 Sift the flour and salt into a bowl and make a well in the centre. Stir in the beer and then add the melted butter and Parmesan mixture. Using a whisk, mix to form a smooth batter. Chill for 2 hours.

3 Just before you are ready to cook the fritters, whisk the egg whites until they form firm peaks and fold them into the batter.

4 Heat the oil in a deep saucepan. Dip the courgette slices into the batter and fry them a few at a time for 3–5 minutes, until golden brown.

5 Remove from the oil, drain on kitchen paper and keep warm while you cook the rest of the courgettes. Serve immediately.

Kevin's Tip

If you don't have a thermostatically controlled deep-fat fryer, remember the following guidelines for deep-frying: don't fill the pan more than a third full with oil; be sure to dry off any excess moisture from whatever you are frying or it will make the oil splutter; test the temperature of the oil by putting in a small cube of bread, which should brown in about 1 minute; fry in small batches so as not to overcrowd the pan.

The range of goats' cheeses available in France never ceases to amaze me and I spend most of my time there trying to decide which is my favourite. **84** The result is always the same – an increased waistline and an awareness that even with two lifetimes I couldn't get around to trying them all!

Salade du Crottin de Polenta Tiède

Grilled Goat's Cheese and Polenta Salad

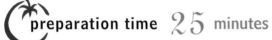 **preparation time** 25 minutes

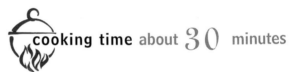 **cooking time** about 30 minutes

 serves 4

 **Ingredients**

125 ml (4 fl oz) olive oil

2 slices of bread, crusts removed, diced

3 tablespoons balsamic vinegar

175 g (6 oz) salad leaves

4 small goats' cheeses or 4 slices from a goat's cheese log

salt and freshly ground black pepper

For the polenta

600 ml (1 pint) water

150 g (5 oz) polenta

25 g (1 oz) butter

1 tablespoon finely chopped fresh dill

75 g (3 oz) Bayonne ham (or any cured ham), diced

a pinch of freshly grated nutmeg

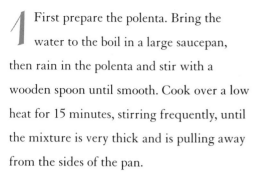

1 First prepare the polenta. Bring the water to the boil in a large saucepan, then rain in the polenta and stir with a wooden spoon until smooth. Cook over a low heat for 15 minutes, stirring frequently, until the mixture is very thick and is pulling away from the sides of the pan.

2 Season with salt and pepper, then stir in the butter, dill, diced ham and nutmeg.

3 Pour the polenta into a buttered baking tray so that it makes a layer about 2.5 cm (1 inch) thick. Leave to cool.

4 Heat 2 tablespoons of the olive oil in a frying pan, add the cubes of bread and fry gently until golden all over. Remove from the pan and set aside.

5 Whisk the remaining olive oil with the balsamic vinegar and some salt and pepper to make a dressing. Put the salad leaves in a bowl, add the croûtons and toss well with the dressing.

6 Using a pastry cutter slightly larger in diameter than the goat's cheese, cut out 4 rounds of polenta. Place them on a baking tray and grill for 3–5 minutes on each side, until golden brown.

7 Sit the goat's cheese on top of the polenta and grill until golden brown.

8 Mound the salad on to 4 serving plates and put the polenta and goat's cheese on top. Serve immediately.

Kevin's Tip

The polenta can be made well in advance as it needs to set before being sliced and grilled. Serve the salad with a good dry white wine – a Chablis or Puligny Montrachet is perfect.

Whether you are served it in a small auberge in northern France, a bistrot in the Midi or a Michelin 3-star establishment on the Côte d'Azur, **86** one thing is for sure: *terrine de campagne* will be full of flavour and texture. This recipe is no exception. Serve with bread, pickles and salad.

Terrine de Campagne
Country Pâté

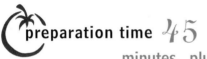 preparation time *45* minutes, plus 24 hours' chilling

 cooking time *2* hours

 serves *10*

Ingredients

3 garlic cloves, crushed

2 bay leaves

125 g (4 oz) onions, finely chopped

12 peppercorns

125 ml (4 fl oz) brandy

5 tablespoons virgin olive oil

2 sprigs of fresh tarragon

2 sprigs of fresh thyme

175 ml (6 fl oz) white wine

175 g (6 oz) gammon, cut into thick strips

250 g (8 oz) veal (you could use pork fillet), cut into thick strips

750 g (1½ lb) boneless, skinless chicken breasts, cut into thick strips

250 g (8 oz) chicken livers

750 g (1½ lb) streaky bacon rashers

250 g (8 oz) raw ham, minced

3 eggs

1 teaspoon dried herbes de Provence

salt and freshly ground black pepper

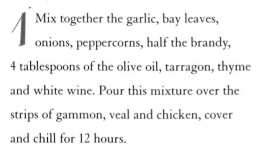

1 Mix together the garlic, bay leaves, onions, peppercorns, half the brandy, 4 tablespoons of the olive oil, tarragon, thyme and white wine. Pour this mixture over the strips of gammon, veal and chicken, cover and chill for 12 hours.

2 Preheat the oven to 180°C, 350°F, gas mark 4.

3 Heat the remaining oil in a frying pan, add the chicken livers and fry for just a few minutes until brown on the outside but still pink on the inside. Remove from the heat and season with salt and pepper.

4 Roughly chop the livers and place them in a bowl. Finely dice 250 g (8 oz) of the bacon and add to the livers with the minced ham, eggs, remaining brandy, herbes de Provence and some salt and black pepper. Mix together thoroughly.

5 Line a 1.5 litre (2 ½ pint) terrine dish with three-quarters of the remaining streaky bacon rashers. Take the bay leaves from the marinade and place them on the base of the terrine. Cover with a quarter of the pâté mixture. Cover with the strips of veal and top with another quarter of the pâté. Arrange the chicken strips on top and cover with pâté, then a layer of gammon and a final layer of pâté. Cover with the remaining bacon rashers. Pour a little of the marinade over the surface.

6 Cover with cling film and aluminium foil, and a lid if there is one. Sit the terrine in a dish of water and cook in the preheated oven for 2 hours.

7 Remove from the oven and place heavy weights on top of the pâté. Leave to cool, then chill for at least 12 hours. Turn out and slice to serve. The terrine will keep for a week in the fridge and can be frozen.

This is my favourite vegetable dish. It makes a wonderful starter and is the tops as a late-night snack served on a toasted plain muffin.

Fricassée de Champignons Sauvages

Casserole of Wild Mushrooms

preparation time
10
minutes

cooking time
about
10
minutes

serves
4

Ingredients

125 g (4 oz) unsalted butter

2 tablespoons vegetable oil

50 g (2 oz) shallots, finely diced

2 garlic cloves, crushed

500 g (1 lb) wild mushrooms, sliced

2 tablespoons chopped fresh coriander

1 tablespoon chopped fresh chives

a pinch of paprika

2 tablespoons vermouth

2 teaspoons French mustard

300 ml (10 fl oz) double cream

25 g (1 oz) fresh Parmesan cheese, grated

salt and freshly ground black pepper

1 Heat the butter and oil in a large frying pan, add the shallots and garlic and cook gently for 5 minutes.

2 Add the mushrooms, coriander, chives and paprika, season with salt and pepper and cook over a medium-high heat for 1 minute, until the mushrooms are golden.

3 Pour in the vermouth, then stir in the mustard and cream. Mix thoroughly and bring to the boil. Check the seasoning and adjust if necessary. Serve straight away, sprinkled with the Parmesan.

This is perhaps the loveliest of all potato dishes but also the most extravagant for both the pocket and the figure.

Gratin Dauphinois

Potatoes Baked in Cream

preparation time *20* minutes

cooking time *40* to *50* minutes

serves *4* to *6*

1 Preheat the oven to 180°C, 350°F, gas mark 4.

2 Put the milk and cream in a pan and bring to the boil. Season with salt, pepper and a good pinch of grated nutmeg.

3 Grease a large gratin dish generously with the butter and sprinkle the garlic over it.

4 Arrange the sliced potatoes in the dish in slightly overlapping layers, seasoning each layer with salt and pepper. Pour the milk and cream over the potatoes.

5 Bake for 40–50 minutes, until the potatoes are tender, and then serve immediately.

Ingredients

200 ml (7 fl oz) milk

200 ml (7 fl oz) double cream

freshly grated nutmeg

75 g (3 oz) softened unsalted butter

4 garlic cloves, crushed

1 kg (2 lb) waxy potatoes, peeled and thinly sliced

salt and freshly ground black pepper

It is hard to imagine a more delectable dish than fresh scallops cooked in this manner. The secret of preparing this recipe is to avoid overcooking them. Serve as a starter or a fish course. Keep it very simple and don't confuse the dish by serving accompaniments such as salad alongside it.

Étuvée de Noix de Saint-Jacques au Fenouil

Butter-braised Scallops with Fennel Sauce

preparation time *30* minutes   cooking time about *10* minutes

serves *4*

Ingredients

8 large fresh scallops	4 teaspoons finely chopped fresh fennel herb
50 g (2 oz) unsalted butter, clarified	125 ml (4 fl oz) dry white wine
2 teaspoons finely chopped fresh fennel herb	50 ml (2 fl oz) vermouth
juice of 1 lemon	1 bay leaf
salt and freshly ground black pepper	350 ml (12 fl oz) double cream
For the sauce	juice of ½ lemon
50 g (2 oz) unsalted butter	4 tomatoes, skinned, deseeded and diced
3 shallots, finely diced	2 tablespoons chopped fresh chives

1 Preheat the oven to 180°C, 350°F, gas mark 4.

2 Remove the scallops from their shells, wash them and gently pat dry. Cut off and discard the small muscle. Using a very sharp knife, slice each scallop horizontally into 3 thin slices.

3 Lightly grease a baking tray with some of the clarified butter. Arrange 3 slices of scallop on the tray so that they overlap slightly and form a circle, brushing each slice with a little of the butter. Repeat with the remaining scallops.

4 Season with salt and pepper, then sprinkle the fennel over the scallops and moisten with the lemon juice. Chill while you make the sauce.

5 Heat the butter in a saucepan, add the shallots and cook gently, without colouring, until softened. Add the chopped fennel, wine, vermouth and bay leaf. Bring to the boil and boil until reduced in volume by half. Stir in the cream and lemon juice and bring to the boil, then season with salt and pepper.

6 Put the scallops into the oven and cook for 2 minutes.

7 Strain the sauce through a fine sieve and flood it over 4 plates. Carefully lift the scallop circles on to the sauce using a large fish slice.

8 Arrange the tomato flesh in 3 little heaps on each plate. Top with the chives and serve immediately.

Kevin's Tip

Scallops are, for me, the king of the sea. If you can obtain them, do try queen scallops, the smaller relation. Slightly sweeter, even tastier, and definitely queen of the sea.

This famous dish from the South of France makes a very substantial main course. It requires three different types of fish and you should not only include your favourite or most economical but put in a little more of one than the other two. It is enriched and thickened with aïoli – a garlic mayonnaise.

Bourride

Creamy Garlic Fish Soup

preparation time
50
minutes

cooking time
about
1
hour

serves
8

Ingredients

2 kg (4½ lb) mixed white fish on the bone, such as cod, haddock and whiting

4 tablespoons olive oil

175 g (6 oz) leeks, chopped

125 g (4 oz) onions, chopped

75 g (3 oz) carrots, chopped

2 garlic cloves, crushed

450 ml (15 fl oz) water

450 ml (15 fl oz) dry white wine

grated zest and juice of 1 lemon

2 tablespoons chopped fresh fennel herb

1 tablespoon chopped fresh thyme

3 bay leaves

a few parsley stalks

1 tablespoon vegetable oil

4 slices of white bread, crusts removed

4 egg yolks

salt and freshly ground black pepper

For the aïoli

2 egg yolks

10 garlic cloves, crushed

300 ml (10 fl oz) extra virgin olive oil

juice of 1 lemon

1 Cut the heads off the fish and discard. Fillet and skin the fish, reserving the trimmings. Cut the flesh into 7.5 cm (3 inch) cubes.

2 Heat the olive oil in a deep pan, add the leeks, onions, carrots and garlic and cook gently for 10 minutes, until softened. Add the fish bones and skin, followed by the water, wine, lemon zest and juice, fennel, thyme and a little salt. Simmer very gently for 25 minutes, skimming any froth off the surface as it develops. Strain into a clean pan.

3 Add the cubed fish to the strained stock with the bay leaves and parsley stalks and cook gently for 5 minutes. Remove the fish from the stock and set aside.

4 Heat the vegetable oil in a frying pan, cut each slice of bread into quarters and fry until golden brown on both sides. Set aside.

5 To make the aïoli, put the 2 egg yolks, garlic, a little salt and some pepper into a food processor and mix to a smooth paste. With the processor at full speed, gradually add the oil, then pour in the lemon juice. Taste and adjust the seasoning with salt and pepper if necessary.

6 Mix 10 tablespoons of the aïoli with the 4 egg yolks. Keep the remaining aïoli in the fridge until required.

7 Bring the stock to the boil, reduce the heat to a simmer and add a small amount of stock to the egg yolk and aïoli mixture. Mix thoroughly and then add this to the remaining stock. Do not let it boil or it will curdle. Stir over a very low heat until it thickens, then remove from the heat and add the fish.

8 Spread the croûtons with aïoli and float them in the soup to serve.

Kevin's Tip

There's a busy little restaurant in Ste Maxime, very close to St Tropez, called La Reserve, where they make the nicest fish soup imaginable.

One of my favourite dishes, this could easily justify the title 'the king of hors d'oeuvre'. The delicate flavour and texture of foie gras is enhanced by the slight tartness of the sauce. If you cannot get hold of duck foie gras you could use chicken livers or even calf's liver instead.

94

Foie Gras à la Crème d'Orange
Foie Gras with an Orange Cream Sauce

preparation time
15
minutes

cooking time
about
20
minutes

serves
4 to *6*

Ingredients

1 fresh duck foie gras, weighing about 500 g (1 lb)

1 garlic clove, crushed

3 shallots, finely diced

1 teaspoon finely crushed green peppercorns

juice and finely grated zest of 2 oranges

1 glass of Cointreau

300 ml (10 fl oz) double cream

25 g (1 oz) unsalted butter, chilled and diced

1 tablespoon chopped fresh coriander

salt and freshly ground black pepper

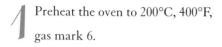
1 Preheat the oven to 200°C, 400°F, gas mark 6.

2 Remove any green surface marks from the foie gras. Separate the lobes and cut them into slices 5 cm (2 inches) thick.

3 Place a large ovenproof frying pan over a high heat. When it is very hot, put the liver in the pan, season with salt and pepper and cook for 1 minute. Turn the liver over, season again and cook for a further minute. Transfer the pan to the oven for 5–8 minutes.

4 Remove the liver from the oven, put it on a warm plate and cover with aluminium foil.

5 Pour off the surplus fat from the frying pan, return it to the hob and add the garlic, shallots, green peppercorns and orange zest. Cook gently for 2 minutes without colouring.

6 Add the orange juice and boil until reduced by half, then pour in the Cointreau. Stir in the cream, bring to the boil and season to taste with salt and pepper.

7 Whisk in the butter a few pieces at a time, then add the chopped coriander. Pour the sauce over the foie gras and serve immediately.

Kevin's Tip

A phenomenal amount of fat comes from foie gras during cooking and it's worth cooling, storing, and using at a later stage for adding an incomparable flavour to soups and stews.

There's a certain rustic element to this dish that symbolizes all that is good about provincial French cooking. You could use hare or even **96** chicken instead of rabbit but be sure to pick a heavy, full-bodied wine. The flesh can alter but the sauce must remain the same.

Lapin en Civet à la Bourgignonne

Burgundy-style Braised Rabbit

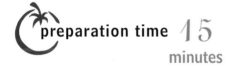

preparation time 15 minutes

cooking time 1 hour

serves 6

Ingredients

4 tablespoons olive oil

25 g (1 oz) butter

1 x 2.25 kg (5 lb) rabbit, skinned and cut into 8–10 pieces

3 garlic cloves, crushed

3 tablespoons chopped fresh coriander

125 g (4 oz) shallots, peeled

125 g (4 oz) button mushrooms

1 bottle of red wine, preferably Burgundy

1 glass of brandy

2 tablespoons tomato purée

1 bouquet garni (1 sprig of thyme, 3 sprigs of parsley, 1 bay leaf, all encased in 2 short lengths of celery and tied with string)

50 g (2 oz) plain flour

50 g (2 oz) softened butter

salt and freshly ground black pepper

1 Heat the oil in a large pan, add the butter and, once it has melted, put the pieces of rabbit in the pan. Season with salt and pepper and cook for 15 minutes, turning frequently, until lightly browned all over.

2 Add the garlic, coriander and the whole shallots and mushrooms. Cook for 5 minutes, then pour in the wine and brandy and add the tomato purée and bouquet garni.

3 Bring slowly to the boil, then turn down the heat, cover and cook gently for 35 minutes, until the rabbit is tender.

4 Mix together the flour and butter to a smooth paste. Remove the rabbit from the sauce and put it in a warmed serving dish. Discard the bouquet garni.

5 Bring the sauce to the boil and add the flour and butter paste a little at a time, whisking vigorously, until the sauce has thickened to a consistency to suit your taste. You may not need all the paste.

6 Check the seasoning and adjust if necessary. Pour the sauce over the rabbit and serve.

Kevin's Tip

Rabbit is a very earthy dish and should be served with accompaniments that enhance not only the flavour but also the texture. Try spring cabbage cooked with juniper berries in a white stock; leeks braised in a rich red wine sauce; or grated carrot stir-fried with a little lemon zest and coriander. Serve with an olive oil, potato and celeriac mash, too, to soak up the juices.

For me, a holiday in France would be incomplete without a soufflé. If you are not a fan of marmalade but like orange, then simply make the dish omitting the marmalade – although I think you will find that its bitterness makes the soufflé very special.

Soufflé à la Marmelade d'Oranges

Orange Marmalade Soufflé

Ingredients

250 ml (8 fl oz) milk

finely grated zest of ½ orange

5 egg yolks

90 g (3½ oz) caster sugar, plus extra for dusting

25 g (1 oz) plain flour

15 g (½ oz) unsalted butter, plus extra for greasing

a little icing sugar

8 egg whites

a pinch of salt

3 tablespoons Grand Marnier

6 tablespoons fine-cut orange marmalade

preparation time

30 minutes

cooking time

30 minutes

serves

6

1 Preheat the oven to 200°C, 400°F, gas mark 6.

2 Lightly grease 6 individual soufflé dishes with soft butter, ensuring that they are evenly coated. Put some caster sugar inside one dish and turn it to coat, then tip the sugar into the next dish. Repeat this process until all the dishes are sugar coated.

3 Put the milk and orange zest into a pan and bring to the boil, then remove from the heat. Whisk 4 of the egg yolks with 50 g (2 oz) of the caster sugar until fluffy. Rain in the flour and whisk for 2 minutes. Pour on half the hot milk, mix together and then pour this mixture into the remaining hot milk.

4 Put the pan back on a very low heat and whisk until it has thickened enough to coat the back of a spoon and has body. Cook gently for 10 minutes, stirring all the time.

5 Pour the mixture into a large bowl and mix in the remaining egg yolk and the butter. Sprinkle a little icing sugar over the surface to prevent a skin forming.

6 Whisk the egg whites with the salt until they form soft peaks. Add the remaining caster sugar and whisk until firm.

7 Lightly whisk a third of the egg white mixture into the soufflé base to loosen it. Using a large metal spoon, gently fold in the remaining egg whites and add the Grand Marnier.

8 Spoon the mixture into the prepared soufflé dishes so that they are half full. Place a spoonful of marmalade in each one and then top up with the rest of the mixture. Wipe away any surplus mixture from the edge of the dishes (this will help the soufflés to rise).

9 Put the dishes in a roasting tin containing a little cold water and bake for 10 minutes. Reduce the temperature to 190°C, 375°F, gas mark 5 and bake for a further 5 minutes, until well risen and golden brown. Remove from the oven, put the soufflé dishes on serving plates and dust the tops with a little icing sugar. Serve immediately.

The French are renowned for their skill at creating the loveliest chocolate desserts. This is without a doubt the king of them all – and extremely rich. Be prepared to work very hard in the gym after eating it.

Tarte au Chocolat

Bitter Chocolate Tart

preparation time

40

minutes, plus 1 hour's chilling

cooking time

1¼ to *1½*

hours

serves

8 to *10*

Ingredients

300 ml (10 fl oz) double cream

175 ml (6 fl oz) milk

500 g (1 lb) best-quality plain chocolate
(at least 70% cocoa solids)

1 egg

2 egg yolks

For the pastry

175 g (6 oz) plain flour

25 g (1 oz) icing sugar

75 g (3 oz) unsalted butter, diced

1 egg yolk

1 tablespoon cold water

1 To make the pastry, sift the flour and sugar together in a bowl, add the butter and rub in with your fingertips to form a sandy mixture.

2 Mix the egg yolk and water together. Make a well in the centre of the flour mixture, add the egg yolk and water, and mix together gently to form a dough. Cover with cling film and chill for 1 hour.

3 Preheat the oven to 200°C, 400°F, gas mark 6.

4 Thinly roll out the pastry on a lightly floured work surface and use to line a deep 20 cm (8 inch) loose-bottomed flan tin. Prick the base with a fork, line with foil or greaseproof paper and fill with baking beans. Bake blind for 10–15 minutes, removing the paper and beans for the last few minutes. Leave on a wire rack to cool. Reduce the oven temperature to 110°C, 225°F, gas mark ¼.

5 For the filling, put the cream and milk in a saucepan and bring to the boil, then remove from the heat and leave to cool.

6 Melt the chocolate in a bowl set over a saucepan of hot water, making sure the water is not touching the base of the bowl. Leave to cool.

7 Whisk the whole egg and egg yolks together until light and fluffy, then stir in the cream and melted chocolate.

8 Pour the filling into the flan case and bake for 60–75 minutes at the reduced oven temperature, until the filling is just set but still moist in the centre. Serve warm.

Kevin's Tip

The key to success here is twofold: first, be sure to take the tart out of the oven when the centre is still slightly sloppy, and secondly, eat it warm. It is at its very best about 1 hour after baking.

I first had this at the Café de Paris in Monte Carlo. It was one of those occasions when you taste a dish and just have to have the recipe – which proved to be the simplest of tasks using the simplest of ingredients. You can serve the ice cream on its own but I like it sandwiched between little sponge biscuits.

Glace à la Noix de Coco

Coconut Ice Cream

preparation time

25

minutes, plus
freezing time

cooking time

6 to 8

minutes

serves

6

*I*ngredients

475 ml (16 fl oz) milk

350 ml (12 fl oz) coconut milk

50 g (2 oz) icing sugar

1 tablespoon brandy

finely grated zest of 2 limes

For the biscuits

50 g (2 oz) unsalted butter

50 g (2 oz) caster sugar

a drop of vanilla extract

a pinch of grated nutmeg

1 large egg white

50 g (2 oz) plain flour

icing sugar for dusting

1 Bring the milk to the boil in a large pan, add the coconut milk and icing sugar and mix well.

2 Strain into a bowl and stir in the brandy and lime zest. Leave to cool, then transfer to an ice-cream maker and freeze until firm.

3 If you don't have an ice-cream maker, pour the mixture into a shallow tray, cover with cling film and place in the freezer. Remove after 30 minutes and stir the mixture with a metal spoon in order to break down ice crystals and ensure that it freezes evenly. Repeat this 3 or 4 times and then freeze until firm.

4 Preheat the oven to 200°C, 400°F, gas mark 6.

5 To make the biscuits, cream together the butter and sugar until light and fluffy. Beat in the vanilla extract and nutmeg.

6 Whisk the egg white until it is stiff enough to hold its shape, then gradually fold it into the butter and sugar mixture. Next fold in the flour.

7 Using 2 teaspoons, place small portions of the mixture on a baking sheet lined with silicone paper, spacing them well apart. Bake for 6–8 minutes, until golden, then transfer to a wire rack to cool.

8 Place a biscuit on each serving plate, cover with a little coconut ice cream, then top with a biscuit. Cover this with more ice cream, then top with another biscuit. Dust with icing sugar and serve straight away. Even lovelier when served with a fresh raspberry coulis.

Kevin's Tip

The biscuits can be made in advance and stored in an airtight container.

France

opposite

Bitter Chocolate Tart 100

Portugal

overleaf (clockwise from top)

Salt Cod Cakes 114

Braised Peas with Smoked Sausage
and Poached Eggs 108

Orange Roulade 122

Portugal

The thing that strikes you about the Portuguese approach to food is its wonderful simplicity and its devotion to really wholesome ingredients. Essentially it is a rustic, family-style cuisine, full of hearty, satisfying dishes. Locals eat loads of beautiful fresh fish, lured to the extensive coastline that traps every species imaginable. Portugal has always been a nation of seafarers and the fishing fleets still provide a large proportion of the country's food supplies, with enough to spare for numerous canning factories along the coast. There are masses of sardines and mountains of cod, much of which is dried and salted. Portugal boasts a different salt cod (*bacalhau*) recipe for every day of the year.

Main dishes are nearly always cooked in olive oil but are never greasy. Instead, they are liberally sprinkled with herbs (always parsley and coriander) and generously spiced. Good news for the reluctant cook – it doesn't take a lot of work in the kitchen to produce delicious food.

It may be ambitious to try and recreate at home the beach-side barbecues of the Algarve coast but, if atmosphere is lacking, you can always try and imagine the setting – swathes of white sandy beaches with a backdrop of spectacular caves, crumbling ochre cliffs, surreal rock formations and coves of translucent water. This is where the great Portuguese seafarers set sail to discover Africa and the route to India, and where nowadays you are guaranteed to taste the finest examples of the famed fish soup. The traditional cooking vessel is as legendary as the recipes – fish soups and succulent clam stews made with the native *presunto* ham are all cooked in the *cataplana* – a clam-shell-shaped device like two woks cobbled together to make a sort of poor man's pressure cooker. The smell of the broth when you lift the clam lid is hard to beat.

It would be fair to say that most countries with access to shellfish produce a prawn soup, but I think this is by far the nicest. Any type of shellfish could be substituted for the prawns but always use fresh and not frozen, as the difference to the finished soup is very noticeable.

Creme de Camarão

Cream of Prawn Soup

 **preparation time**
40
minutes

 **cooking time** about
45
minutes

 serves
6

 *I*ngredients

750 g (1½ lb) raw, shell-on prawns	4 tomatoes, skinned, deseeded and chopped
1.5 litres (2½ pints) water	1 glass of dry white wine
3 tablespoons olive oil	a pinch of sugar
125 g (4 oz) leeks, diced	125 ml (4 fl oz) vegetable oil
75 g (3 oz) onions, diced	6 slices of bread, crusts removed, cut into small cubes
3 garlic cloves, crushed	
3 tablespoons chopped fresh coriander	1 tablespoon finely chopped fresh flat-leaf parsley
1 bay leaf	150 ml (5 fl oz) double cream
50 g (2 oz) tomato purée	salt and freshly ground black pepper

1 Put the prawns into a large saucepan, add the water and bring slowly to the boil. Remove from the heat and drain, reserving the water. Leave the prawns to cool, then shell them, reserving the shells, and remove the black vein running along the back of each one.

2 Heat the olive oil in a clean pan, add the leeks, onions and garlic and cook gently for 5 minutes.

3 Add the prawn shells to the vegetables and cook for 2 minutes. Stir in the coriander, bay leaf, tomato purée, tomatoes, white wine and sugar. Mix together, then add the prawn cooking liquid. Season lightly with salt and pepper, bring to the boil, then reduce the heat and simmer gently for 30 minutes.

4 Put half the prawns in a food processor and process until very finely chopped, then stir them into the soup.

5 Heat the vegetable oil in a frying pan, add the cubes of bread and cook until golden brown all over. Remove from the pan and drain on kitchen paper. Season with a little salt and dust with the parsley.

6 Strain the soup into a clean pan, add the cream and bring slowly to the boil. Stir in the remaining whole prawns. Check the seasoning and adjust if necessary. Serve with the croûtons scattered over the soup.

Kevin's Tip

This makes a perfect dinner party starter. It can be made the day before, cooled and then refrigerated overnight. Do be sure to reheat it thoroughly. You could be very wicked and top the soup with aïoli (see page 92).

This is the Portuguese answer to Comfort Cuisine – fresh peas and smoked sausage served as a starter, main course, accompaniment or simply a snack. It's one of the most versatile recipes around and produces a flavour-packed dish at a very economical price.

Paio com Ervilhas

Braised Peas with Smoked Sausage and Poached Eggs

preparation time
10
minutes

cooking time
20
minutes

serves *4*
as a starter or
accompaniment, *2*
as a main course

Ingredients

75 g (3 oz) butter

75 g (3 oz) onions, finely diced

1 garlic clove, crushed

150 ml (5 fl oz) chicken stock

500 g (1 lb) shelled peas

2 tablespoons chopped fresh parsley

250 g (8 oz) *paio* (cooked smoked sausage), sliced

1 tablespoon white wine vinegar

4 eggs

salt and freshly ground black pepper

1 Melt the butter in a shallow pan, add the onions and garlic and cook gently for 5 minutes without letting them brown.

2 Add the chicken stock, peas and parsley. Season with salt and pepper, then cover the pan and cook gently for 5 minutes.

3 Add the sliced sausage and cook for a further 5 minutes. Check to ensure that the peas are cooked. If not, then simmer for a few minutes longer.

4 Meanwhile bring a large, fairly shallow pan of water to a simmer and add the vinegar and some salt. Poach the eggs in the water, then remove with a slotted spoon and drain on kitchen paper.

5 Transfer the pea and sausage mixture to a warmed serving dish, top with the poached eggs and serve immediately.

Kevin's Tip

Of all the Portuguese sausages by far the best, in my opinion, are the paio, *even though the* chourico *is more widely acknowledged as the Portuguese favourite. The flavour of both of these sausages is very similar but the* paio *is made with loin of pork rather than fat pork, there are chunks of the meat in the sausage and they are much thicker than the* chourico. *If you find it impossible to obtain these then use any heavily spiced sausage.*

I first tasted this salad in Val de Lobo in the Algarve and was struck by the intensity of its flavours. This is achieved by lightly roasting the

tomatoes and peppers. Given that they have had a head start with all that sunshine, this added twist makes them release even more flavour.

Salada à Portuguesa

Portuguese Salad

preparation time
15
minutes

cooking time
10
minutes

serves
6

Ingredients

4 green peppers, halved and deseeded

2 tablespoons vegetable oil

5 tomatoes

125 g (4 oz) cucumber, peeled and thinly sliced

2 garlic cloves, crushed

4 tablespoons extra virgin olive oil

2 tablespoons balsamic vinegar

3 tablespoons chopped fresh basil

salt and freshly ground black pepper

1 Put the peppers skin-side up on a baking sheet and brush them with a little of the vegetable oil. Place under a hot grill until the skin bubbles and blackens, then leave to cool.

2 Brush the tomatoes with the remaining vegetable oil and grill until the skin bubbles and burns. Peel off the skin from the green peppers and the tomatoes.

3 Slice the peppers and put them in a bowl. Cut the tomatoes in half and remove the seeds. Slice the tomato flesh thickly and add to the peppers.

4 Add the cucumber and garlic to the bowl and season very lightly with salt and pepper.

5 Mix together the olive oil and balsamic vinegar and use to dress the salad, then scatter over the chopped basil.

Kevin's Tip

Lightly roasting vegetables in order to develop the full flavour is a great technique that works every time. Mushrooms in particular benefit enormously from a few minutes either under the grill or in a hot oven before being added to a sauce or soup.

A deep dish that can be placed on the hob and then transferred to the table is ideal for this recipe. Originally it was made in a kettle-like dish known as a *cataplana*, which allowed the flavours to develop as much as possible while the ingredients settled under and over the mussels.

Mexilhões na Cataplana

Mussels with Garlic Sausage Cooked in a Kettle

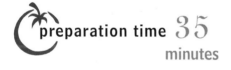 preparation time 35 minutes

 cooking time 15 to 20 minutes

 serves 6

Ingredients

48 mussels	a pinch of paprika
3 tablespoons olive oil	a pinch of cayenne pepper
125 g (4 oz) garlic sausage, cut into cubes	a pinch of crushed dried chilli
75 g (3 oz) prosciutto, trimmed and diced	1 bay leaf
175 g (6 oz) onions, finely chopped	750 g (1½ lb tomatoes), skinned, deseeded and sliced
4 garlic cloves, crushed	150 ml (5 fl oz) dry white wine
1 red pepper, deseeded and sliced	4 tablespoons chopped fresh dill

1 Scrub the mussels under coid running water. Pull off the beards and scrape off any barnacles with a small sharp knife. Discard any open mussels that do not close when tapped lightly on a work surface.

2 Heat the oil in a large deep saucepan, add the garlic sausage and prosciutto and cook gently for 1 minute. Add the onions, garlic and red pepper and cook for 2 minutes.

3 Sprinkle in the paprika, cayenne and chilli, then add the bay leaf, tomatoes and white wine. Bring to the boil and season with salt and pepper.

4 Pour half the mixture into the serving dish. Place the mussels on top and spread the rest of the tomato mixture over them. Cover with a tight-fitting lid and cook gently for 10–15 minutes, then remove the lid and check that the shells have opened. If not, then cook for a few minutes longer.

5 Discard any mussels that have not opened. Check the seasoning and adjust if necessary, then garnish with the chopped dill and serve straight away. Be sure to provide a finger bowl of warm water.

Kevin's Tip

A great proportion of the mussels sold today will have been reared in purified water. Whilst it is the view of some traditionalists that mussels produced this way develop less flavour they will all agree that the mussels need less cleaning. The general rules for buying mussels are the same as for all shellfish: buy from a reputable dealer, store in the fridge until ready to use them – which should be the same day as purchase – and check and discard any dead ones prior to cooking.

Probably one of Portugal's best-known dishes, this is found everywhere from exclusive restaurants to inexpensive tavernas. If you cannot obtain

salt cod, available from Portuguese and West Indian delicatessens, then you could substitute fresh cod or hake and salt it yourself.

Pastéis de Bacalhau

Salt Cod Cakes

preparation time *40* minutes,
plus 24 hours' soaking

cooking time about
50
minutes

serves
6
as a main course

Ingredients

350 g (12 oz) salt cod

500 g (1 lb) potatoes

3 eggs, beaten

25 g (1 oz) butter, melted

125 g (4 oz) spring onions, finely chopped

2 tablespoons roughly
chopped fresh parsley

vegetable oil for deep-frying

salt and freshly ground black pepper

1 Soak the salt cod in plenty of cold water for 24 hours, changing the water several times.

2 Wash the potatoes and boil them until tender, then drain well. Peel and mash the potatoes.

3 Drain the cod, put it in a pan with just enough water to cover and poach until tender. Drain, then remove the skin and any bones. Using a fork, flake the fish into small pieces.

4 Put the fish in a bowl with the mashed potatoes, eggs, melted butter, spring onions and parsley. Mix together thoroughly. Taste and, if necessary, season with salt and pepper, then leave to cool.

5 Mould the mixture into 12 egg-shaped cakes. Heat the vegetable oil in a deep pan and fry the fish cakes a few at a time for 5–6 minutes, until golden brown.

6 Drain the fish cakes on kitchen paper and then serve straight away, with a dressed salad.

Kevin's Tip

I have to confess that before I visited Portugal I was not a great lover of salt cod but this dish uses it to its best advantage. The full flavour of the fish is developed and this has become a favourite snack in my house. Do be sure to soak the cod thoroughly in several changes of water, otherwise it will still be too salty.

This dish owes its name to the terracotta pot in which the chicken used to be cooked. These days you are more likely to find it served in a modern casserole dish. Irrespective of what it's cooked in, the ham and pork add a wonderful flavour dimension to the chicken.

Frango na Pucra

Jugged Chicken

preparation time
40
minutes

cooking time
2 to *2¼*
hours

serves
4

Ingredients

1 x 1.6 kg (3½ lb) chicken	1 tablespoon tomato purée
4 tablespoons extra virgin olive oil	300 ml (10 fl oz) dry white wine
8 button onions, peeled	150 ml (5 fl oz) port
4 garlic cloves, peeled	1 tablespoon Meaux-type mustard
50 g (2 oz) fresh flat-leaf parsley	50 g (2 oz) stoned black olives
125 g (4 oz) cured ham	chopped fresh coriander, to garnish
1 bay leaf	salt and freshly ground black pepper
6 tomatoes, skinned, deseeded and chopped	

1 Preheat the oven to 180°C, 350°F, gas mark 4.

2 Season the chicken very lightly with salt and pepper, and brush with the olive oil. Put half the button onions, garlic cloves and parsley into the cavity of the bird and secure with string or trussing sticks. (This will help the bird keep its shape and enhance the flavour during cooking.)

3 Arrange half the cured ham over the base of a deep ovenproof dish with the remaining parsley, onions and garlic and the bay leaf. Sit the chicken on top and cover the breasts with the remaining cured ham.

4 Mix together the tomatoes, tomato purée, wine, port and mustard. Season with salt and pepper and pour it over the chicken. Cover with a tight-fitting lid.

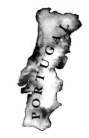

5 Bake in the preheated oven for 1¾–2 hours, until the chicken is tender (the juices should run clear when the thigh is pierced with a skewer near the bone). Carefully transfer the chicken to a roasting tray and keep it warm in the switched-off oven.

6 Bring the sauce to the boil on the hob and boil until reduced by at least a third. Check the seasoning and adjust if necessary.

7 Dissect the bird, display neatly on a serving dish and pour the sauce over. Garnish with the black olives and some chopped coriander.

Kevin's Tip

I like to serve celeriac and potato mash with this dish. Just boil peeled celeriac and potatoes until tender, then drain and mash. Drizzle in enough olive oil to give a slightly runny mixture, season and stir in some chopped fresh coriander.

I persuaded the chef of a restaurant in Lisbon to divulge this recipe. He spoke Portuguese and I spoke English but we both understood each **118** other – amazing really! The dish needs to be prepared about 24 hours before cooking.

Costeleta de Porco a Massa de Pimento

Pork Chops with a Sweet Pepper Paste

preparation time
25
minutes, plus 6 hours' chilling and 12 hours' marinating

cooking time
about
2 ¹/₂
hours

serves
4

Ingredients

4 red peppers, deseeded and halved

1 tablespoon coarse salt

2 garlic cloves, crushed

75 ml (3 fl oz) extra virgin olive oil

4 pork chops

150 ml (5 fl oz) dry white wine

4 tablespoons olive oil

salt and freshly ground black pepper

1 Arrange a layer of the peppers in a small earthenware dish. Cover with a little of the salt and repeat this process so that you finish with 5 layers of peppers. Chill for 6 hours.

2 Preheat the oven to 120°C, 250°F, gas mark ½.

3 Bake the peppers in the oven for 2 hours, until soft, then remove and leave to cool.

4 Skin the peppers and then put them in a food processor with the garlic and blend to a smooth paste. Slowly add the extra virgin olive oil, blending constantly, and season with a little black pepper. The paste can be stored in an airtight container in the fridge if made in advance.

5 Coat both sides of the pork chops with the pepper paste and place them in a shallow dish. Pour over the wine, cover and chill for 12 hours.

6 Heat the oil in a griddle or a heavy-based frying pan. Cook the chops for 4–5 minutes per side, until lightly browned, then remove from the pan and keep warm.

7 Pour the marinade into the pan and boil until it has reduced in volume by a third. Return the pork chops to the pan and cook for 5 minutes. Check the seasoning and adjust if necessary, then serve.

Kevin's Tip

The sweet pepper paste works just as well with other meats besides pork. The chops are lovely served with deep-fried aubergines and a tomato and basil salad.

I would suggest serving this fiery sauce with a plate of barbecued king pra
sardines and scallops, along with a well-dressed salad and plenty of boiled

𝓡ed Pepper Sauce

𝓜olho de 𝓟iri 𝓟iri

preparation time
15
minutes

cooking time
10
minutes

serves
4

1 Preheat the oven to 190°C, 375°F, gas mark 5.

2 Roast the chillies in the oven for 10 minutes. Leave until cool enough to handle and then peel off the skins with a small sharp knife.

3 Put all the ingredients in a food processor and process to a paste. Alternatively, chop the chillies and garlic very finely and then whisk together with all the remaining ingredients in a bowl.

4 Store in an airtight jar in the fridge. The sauce will keep for about 4 weeks.

𝓘ngredients

3–8 red chillies, according to taste

1 garlic clove, peeled

150 ml (5 fl oz) olive oil

4 tablespoons white wine vinegar

salt

𝓚evin's Tip

The piri piri peppers originally used for this sauce came from Brazil. However, you can use any type of chilli – more chillies, more heat!

While this uses near-identical ingredients to British rice pudding the method is quite different, more like making risotto.

Arroz Doze

Rice Pudding

preparation time
15
minutes

cooking time about
45
minutes

serves
6 to *8*

Ingredients

500 g (1 lb) short grain rice, washed and drained

finely grated zest of ½ lemon

1.2 litres (2 pints) milk

250 g (8 oz) granulated sugar

4 egg yolks

a pinch of salt

15 g (½ oz) unsalted butter

ground cinnamon

1 Put the rice in a measuring jug and check the level, then pour it into another container. Measure 2½ times its volume of water, pour the water into a large pan and bring to the boil. Add the rice and lemon zest, reduce the heat and simmer for 12–15 minutes, until the water has been absorbed.

2 Over a low heat, add the milk a ladleful at a time, stirring constantly with a wooden spoon and allowing the rice to absorb the milk before adding more.

3 With the last of the milk, add the sugar, egg yolks, salt, butter and a pinch of cinnamon. Mix well, cover with a tight-fitting lid and cook very gently for 15–20 minutes.

4 Serve hot, with a little cinnamon sprinkled over the surface, or chilled.

In a country where oranges are as fresh as a northeastern British winter, I think that this is one of the nicest ways to use them. It is a fairly unusual roulade in that it does not include flour. The result is surprising, as the pudding is quite heavy in both flavour and body.

Torta de Laranja

Orange Roulade

preparation time
25
minutes

cooking time
10 to 15
minutes

serves
4

Ingredients

150 g (5 oz) caster sugar

3 large eggs

juice and finely grated zest of 1 orange

a pinch of allspice

fresh orange segments, to serve

Kevin's Tip

When feeling really wicked, before rolling up the roulade I like to spread it with a little marmalade and then top that with lightly whipped cream that has been flavoured with a little caster sugar and vanilla extract. But only when I'm feeling really wicked!

1 Preheat the oven to 220°C, 425°F, gas mark 7.

2 Put half the sugar in a bowl, add the eggs and, preferably with an electric whisk, beat for at least 4 minutes, until the mixture is thick and full bodied and leaves a trail on the surface when drizzled from the whisk.

3 Fold in the orange juice and zest and the allspice.

4 Transfer the mixture to a 37.5 x 25 x 2.5 cm (15 x 10 x 1 inch) baking tray lined with greased and floured silicone paper, spreading the mixture out evenly. Bake for 10–15 minutes, until the surface of the cake is golden brown.

5 Place a tea towel on a work surface and lay a sheet of greaseproof paper on top. Sprinkle the remaining sugar over the greaseproof paper.

6 Loosen the edges of the cake with a sharp knife. Carefully tip the cake upside down on to the sugar-covered paper and lift the baking tray off. Gently peel the lining paper from the base of the cake, then lift one end of the tea towel, gripping it tightly, and use it to help roll up the cake. Leave to cool.

7 Cut the cake into slices and serve accompanied by fresh orange segments, and a little cream or ice cream if you like.

These delightful little biscuits are very easy to make and can be served with a cup of coffee, or even alongside a chunk of cheese.

Bolos de Pinhões

Pine Nut Biscuits

 **preparation time** *15* minutes

 **cooking time** *8* to *10* minutes

 makes *30*

 **Ingredients**

175g (6 oz) pine nuts

125 g (4 oz) cornflour

65 g (2½ oz) plain flour

75 g (3 oz) butter, melted

125 g (4 oz) caster sugar

4 small eggs, beaten

a pinch of ground cinnamon

a pinch of salt

1 Preheat the oven to 220°C, 425°F, gas mark 7.

2 Crush the pine nuts, but not too finely, with a mortar and pestle or in a food processor or electric grinder. Sift the cornflour and flour into a large bowl and stir in the pine nuts.

3 Mix together the melted butter, sugar, eggs, cinnamon and salt. Pour on to the dry ingredients and knead lightly to form a dough.

4 Shape the mixture into small balls and flatten them gently with your hand to make biscuits about 7.5 cm (3 inches) in diameter.

5 Place on a baking tray lined with silicone paper and bake for 8–10 minutes, until golden brown. Cool on a wire rack and then store in an airtight container.

The Algarve grows the most wonderful sweet potatoes and these little cakes are an unusual way of preparing them.

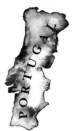

Tartes de Batata

Sweet Potato Cakes

preparation time *40* minutes   **makes** *30*

cooking time *10* to *12* minutes

Ingredients

350 g (12 oz) granulated sugar

75 g (3 oz) butter, melted

500 g (1 lb) sweet potatoes, cooked and mashed

25 g (1 oz) plain flour

75 g (3 oz) ground almonds

50 g (2 oz) glacé cherries

a pinch of ground cinnamon

3 tablespoons orange juice

finely grated zest of ½ orange

caster sugar for dusting

1 Preheat the oven to 190°C, 375°F, gas mark 5.

2 Mix the sugar with 50 g (2 oz) of the melted butter, then add the mashed potatoes, flour, ground almonds, glacé cherries, cinnamon, orange juice and zest, and mix together well.

3 Put the mixture into a saucepan and heat until the excess liquid has boiled away. Remove from the heat and turn out on to a lightly floured surface.

4 Shape the mixture into small rounds the size of 50p pieces, about 2.5 cm (1 inch) thick. Place them on a lightly greased baking sheet and brush with the remaining butter.

5 Bake for 10–12 minutes, until golden brown, then remove from the oven and dust with caster sugar.

Index of recipe titles in native language

Greece
Domátes yemistes 10
Taramosalata 12
Horiátiki 13
Mithia tiganitá 14
Sarthelles sto foúrno 16
Melitzánes sto foúrno 18
Spanakotyropitta 20
Dolmathakiá latherá 22
Kalamárakia yemistá 24
Soutzoukákia smyrneiká 26
Sfougáto 28
Karpópitta me méli 30

Italy
Zuppa di fagioli 60
Crostini con salmone affumicato 61
Piadini con spinaci 62
Risotto al pomodoro e basilica 64
Zucchine alla parmigiana 66
Melanzane al forno 68
Stufato di pollo e targone 70
Braciole 72
Vitello alla mozzarella 74
Pasta fresca 76
Tiramisù 77
Souffle di amaretto gelato 78

Portugal
Creme de camarão 106
Paio com ervilhas 108
Salada à Portuguesa 110
Mexilhões na cataplana 112
Pastéis de bacalhau 114
Frango na pucra 116
Costeleta de porco a massa de
    pimento 118
Molho de piri piri 120
Arroz doze 121
Torta de laranja 122
Bolos de pinhões 124
Tartes de batata 125

Spain
Sopa de pescado 34
Empanadas Valencianas 36
Peperrada 38
Tumbret 40
Fideos con almejas 42
Paella a la marinera 44
Pollo en pepitoria 46
Chuletos de cerdo en salsa de
    Granadas 48
Arroz rosetxat 50
Buñuelos de viento 52
Crema Catalana 54
Torta de platanos 56

France
Beignets de courgettes au parmesan 82
Salade du crottin de polenta tiède 84
Terrine de campagne 86
Fricassée de champignons sauvages 88
Gratin dauphinois 89
Etuvée de noix de Saint-Jacques au
    fenouil 90
Bourride 92
Foie gras à la crème d'orange 94
Lapin en civet à la Bourgignonne 96
Soufflé à la marmelade d'oranges 98
Tarte au chocolat 100
Glace à la noix de coco 102

Index